PRELIMINARY REPORT

CONCERNING

EXPLORATIONS AND SURVEYS

PRINCIPALLY IN

NEVADA AND ARIZONA.

PRELIMINARY REPORT

CONCERNING

EXPLORATIONS AND SURVEYS

PRINCIPALLY IN

NEVADA AND ARIZONA.

PROSECUTED IN ACCORDANCE WITH PARAGRAPH 2, SPECIAL ORDERS
No. 109, WAR DEPARTMENT, MARCH 18, 1871, AND LETTER
OF INSTRUCTIONS OF MARCH 23, 1871,

FROM

BRIGADIER GENERAL A. A. HUMPHREYS,
CHIEF OF ENGINEERS.

CONDUCTED UNDER THE IMMEDIATE DIRECTION OF

1st Lieut. GEORGE M. WHEELER, Corps of Engineers.

BOOKS FOR LIBRARIES PRESS
FREEPORT, NEW YORK

First Published 1872
Reprinted 1970

INTERNATIONAL STANDARD BOOK NUMBER:
0-8369-5590-0

LIBRARY OF CONGRESS CATALOG CARD NUMBER:
70-137389

PRINTED IN THE UNITED STATES OF AMERICA

TABLE OF CONTENTS.

WAR DEPARTMENT, *April* 19, 1872.

The Secretary of War has the honor to transmit to the United States Senate a preliminary report of Lieutenant George M. Wheeler, Corps of Engineers, of the progress of the engineer exploration of the public domain in Nevada and Arizona, which, it is believed, will satisfactorily meet the request contained in the Senate resolution of the 7th ultimo, and to invite the attention of that body to the estimate of funds necessary for the continuance of the work, embraced in the letter of the Chief of Engineers forwarding the report, for which purpose no provision was made in the regular estimate for appropriations heretofore made to Congress.

WM. W. BELKNAP,
Secretary of War.

OFFICE OF THE CHIEF OF ENGINEERS,
Washington, D. C., April 18, 1872.

SIR: In compliance with the following resolution of the Senate of the United States, "That the Secretary of War be requested to communicate, for the information of the Senate, a report showing the present condition of the explorations now being conducted under the direction of the Engineer Department, (in Nevada and Arizona,) and in the immediate charge of Lieutenant George M. Wheeler, Corps of Engineers," I have the honor to submit herewith a preliminary report from Lieutenant Wheeler, which, it is believed, will furnish all the information contemplated in the resolution. The preliminary topographical map referred to in the report has just been completed, and two copies are transmitted herewith.

I desire to invite attention to the extent of country in the interior that has not yet been explored instrumentally, and to recommend to favorable consideration the project and estimate submitted by Lieutenant Wheeler for continuing the exploration of these unknown areas.

For the next season's work the sum of $75,000 is necessary.

The early mapping of this region will be of great service not only for governmental purposes, but in furnishing information eagerly sought for by those interested in mining and other industrial pursuits.

　　　　Very respectfully, your obedient servant,

　　　　　　　　　　　　　　　　　A. A. HUMPHREYS,
　　　　　　　　　　　　　　Brigadier General and Chief of Engineers.

Hon. WM. W. BELKNAP,
　　　　Secretary of War.

PRELIMINARY REPORT

OF

EXPLORATIONS IN NEVADA AND ARIZONA.

By GEO. M. WHEELER,

First Lieutenant Corps of Engineers.

UNITED STATES ENGINEER OFFICE,
(EXPLORATIONS IN NEVADA AND ARIZONA,)
Washington, D. C., March 19, 1872.

GENERAL: I have the honor to forward, in acknowledgment of your communication of the 12th instant, a preliminary report, with appendices, presenting, so far as circumstances will permit, such of the results relating to the explorations of the past season, (as are liable to be soonest needed,) and explanations regarding the present condition of our labors, thinking that this will in the best manner satisfy the spirit of the resolution of the Senate of the 8th instant, a copy ot which you inclose. It will also supply, in a measure, the part of a more detailed annual report, that should have been forwarded from the field only for the great urgency of other duties; and your attention is called to some of the suggestions in favor of a continuance of explorations in the field of our western territory, and to the estimates presented. A preliminary topographical map, now nearly completed, will be forwarded at the earliest opportunity.

All of which is respectfully submitted.

GEO. M. WHEELER,
First Lieutenant, Corps of Engineers, in charge of
Explorations in Nevada and Arizona.

Brigadier General A. A. HUMPHREYS,
Chief of Engineers U. S. Army, Washington, D. C.

2

INTRODUCTION.

In presenting this preliminary report, it has been deemed advisable to divide it into two separate parts, the first giving the localities included in the survey, some general details, and an average of the cost, based upon the area traversed; the second giving, as plainly as circumstances permit, the present condition of the results from this work.

The following are copies of the special orders from the War Department:

Special Orders }
No. 109.—Extract. }
WAR DEPARTMENT, ADJUTANT GENERAL'S OFFICE,
Washington, March 18, 1871.

*   *   *   *   *   *   *   *

2. Upon the recommendation of the Chief of Engineers, 1st Lieutenant George M. Wheeler, Corps of Engineers, is hereby assigned to the charge of the exploration, under the direction of the Chief of Engineers, of those portions of the United States territory lying south of the Central Pacific Railroad, embracing parts of Eastern Nevada and Arizona.

The Quartermaster General will, in addition to the transportation and supply of the escort, procure the necessary animals and forage them *en route.* He will furnish transportation from the East to San Francisco, and thence to the field, for the civilian assistants of Lieutenant Wheeler, and the subsistence stores, instruments, &c.

The Commissary General of Subsistence will furnish the necessary rations and anti-scorbutics for the party.

The Surgeon General will furnish one medical officer and two hospital stewards, and the necessary medical stores.

The Chief of Ordnance will supply horse equipments, arms, and ammunition at such points as may be necessary.

*   *   *   *   *   *   *   *

By order of the Secretary of War:

E. D. TOWNSEND,
Adjutant General.

Special Orders }
No. 110.—Extract. }
HEADQUARTERS OF THE ARMY, ADJUTANT GENERAL'S OFFICE,
Washington, March 18, 1871.

*   *   *   *   *   *   *   *

2. The Commanding General Military Division of the Pacific will furnish proper escort to the exploration party referred to in Special Orders No. 109, of this date, from the War Department, for the exploration of those portions of the United States territory lying south of the Central Pacific Railroad, embracing points of Eastern Nevada and Arizona.

*   *   *   *   *   *   *   *

By command of General Sherman:

E. D. TOWNSEND,
Adjutant General.

The general plan to be pursued was indicated in the letter of instructions of the Chief of Engineers, dated March 23, 1871, and was only modified as imperative circumstances required. The following is a copy of the letter of instructions mentioned:

OFFICE OF THE CHIEF OF ENGINEERS,
Washington, D. C., March 23, 1871.

SIR: The Secretary of War, in his orders of March 18, 1871, a copy of which has been furnished you, has assigned you to the charge of the exploration, under the direction of the Chief of Engineers, of those portions of the United States territory lying south of the Central Pacific Railroad, embracing parts of Eastern Nevada and Arizona.

The main object of this exploration will be to obtain correct topographical knowledge of the country traversed by your parties, and to prepare accurate maps of that section. In making this the main object, it is at the same time intended that you ascertain as far as practicable everything relating to the physical features of the country, the numbers, habits, and disposition of the Indians who may live in this section, the selection of such sites as may be of use for future military operations or occupation, and the facilities offered for making rail or common roads, to meet the wants of those who at some future period may occupy or traverse this part of our territory.

In ascertaining the physical features, your attention is particularly called to the mineral resources that may be discovered, and, where the indications would seem to justify it, you should have minute and detailed examinations made of the locality and character of the deposits.

The influence of climate, the geological formations, character and kinds of vegetation, its probable value for agricultural and grazing purposes, relative proportions of woodland, water, and other qualities, which affect its value for the settler, should be carefully observed.

The latitude and longitude of as many as possible of the important points should be accurately determined, and in order to assist you in this, it is suggested that you make arrangements with the officers in charge of the United States Lake Survey and United States Naval Observatory, so as to determine by telegraph the longitude of those points nearest your field of labor, with which your field-work can be connected.

To accomplish these objects most effectually, you will divide your expedition into two parts, and have both parties start from points to the west of Elko Station, proceeding in a southerly direction ; meet at or near Belmont ; following the same plan and direction leaving Belmont, meet at Camp Independence, in California. Leaving Camp Independence, following a southeasterly direction, they will meet at or near Stump Springs, on the old Salt Lake road. Upon arriving at this point, you will organize a party to go to Fort Mohave, and using the boats already stored there, make an examination of the Colorado River as far as the crossing of the old Santa Fé trail, where they will be met by the main expedition. The boat party will continue to examine the Colorado River, as far as practicable, while the main party will camp at Peacock's Spring. Leaving Peacock's Spring after the junction of the parties, the expedition will divide as before ; diverging from this station, will come together at Prescott, Arizona Territory. Hence making an examination of the country on both sides of the San Francisco Mountains, when the field-labor may be terminated.

The following places are designated as convenient for depots, viz : Camp Independence, California ; Camps Mohave, Hualapais, Whipple, and Apache, in Arizona ; and Camps Wingate and Bayard, in New Mexico.

You will use your own judgment in modifying the plan proposed in the event of any unforeseen circumstances or physical obstacles preventing an adherence to it.

To aid you in the discharge of these duties, Lieutenant D. W. Lockwood, of the Corps of Engineers, has been ordered to report to you, and you are authorized to employ ten assistants as topographers, geologists, naturalists, &c., at salaries already authorized from this office in letters of previous date ; also, the necessary number of packers, guides, and laborers, to complete your party. The whole number of civilian employés not to exceed thirty in number. You will procure your assistants, employés, equipments, supplies, &c., at those points which seem to insure the most economical and effective organization for the party, and are authorized to pay their actual transportation to and from, and to subsist them while in, the field.

You will make requisition on this office for such instruments as you may require, and are authorized to purchase one spring-wagon for transporting the astronomical instruments, sextants, chronometers, and magnetic instruments for the use of the expedition.

All necessary transportation, provisions, supplies, &c., which you cannot obtain from the supply departments of the Army, and books, stationery, and drawing materials, will be paid for from the funds in your hands.

You will communicate with this office as often as the means of communication will allow, forwarding the usual reports and returns required by the regulations, and such other reports as will keep this office apprised of your movements, and the progress of the expedition under your charge.

The sum of $50,000 has been set apart to meet your expenses until June 30, 1872, and you are particularly requested to be economical in your disbursements, and under no circumstances to exceed this amount. On the completion of your field duty you will dispose of the public property in your charge, discharge such assistants and employés of your party for whom you have no further need, and return to Washington to make your report and prepare the necessary maps.

Very respectfully, your obedient servant,

A. A. HUMPHREYS,
Brigadier General, and Chief of Engineers.

Lieutenant GEORGE M. WHEELER,
Corps of Engineers, Washington, D. C.

In accordance with telegraphic orders from the War Department, dated March 11, and as mentioned in letter of instructions from the Chief of Engineers of March 23, 1871, Lieutenant D. W. Lockwood, Corps of Engineers, was to have assisted in the performance of the duties of the exploration ; but, owing to some misapprehension on the part of the commanding officer of the department in which Lieutenant Lockwood was serving, he was not able to enter upon his labors until early in August. This single matter, because of the incident vexatious delays occasioned by the multiple nature of the duties thrust upon my shoulders, was the reason for the loss of nearly one month in time before the parties could be said to have fairly organized for systematic work. This caused serious inconvenience through the entire season, and it often seemed almost certain that, in consequence, the entire field of the labor projected could not be finished prior to the setting in of the winter.

Second Lieutenant D. A. Lyle, Second United States Artillery, who had been serving with his company in Alaska, was, at my request, ordered to join the expedition, but was unable to reach any of the rendezvous camps until that one established at Belmont, Nevada, a little prior to July 1, when he was at once placed in charge of main party No. 2 and the escort. He performed this latter duty until the close of the season's operations, and in many ways allied himself with the professional undertakings of the exploration.

The Medical Department was to furnish one surgeon and two hospital stewards. These persons came from the Military Division of the Pacific, and were as follows: Acting Assistant Surgeon A. H. Cochrane; Hospital Stewards Frank Hecox and T. V. Brown, the latter joining the command at Halleck Station, Nevada. Subsequently, Acting Assistant Surgeon Walter J. Hoffman reported at Carlin, Nevada, having been appointed by the honorable Secretary of War at the instance of Professor S. F. Baird, of the Smithsonian Institution, and upon the recommendation of the Surgeon General. He was at once placed in charge of the departments of mineralogy and natural history. Dr. Cochrane performed the duties of "surgeon to the expedition," while the two hospital stewards accomplished excellent services as meteorological observers.

The areas intended to be examined were entirely, with the exception of certain small sections, in Southwestern Utah, within the limits of the Military Division of the Pacific, and the furnishing of the escort was effected through the commanding general, whose kindness in this as well as in all matters relating to the supplies and furthering the objects of the expedition was constantly evinced. The permanent escort that continued with the expedition until its termination came from Troop I, Third United States Cavalry, and consisted of two sergeants, four corporals, and twenty-six privates, then serving in the Department of California, Brigadier General E. O. C. Ord commanding, to whom, for his generous aid and counsel at this time, as well as at all others, I feel especially grateful. Other temporary escorts were obtained from several of the posts in Arizona, and Lieutenant Colonel George Crook, commanding this department at the time of our entering its limits, was very kind in authorizing the facilities asked for in our informal requisitions.

No lieutenant of cavalry was available to be placed in charge of the escort, as the troops of the Third Cavalry at Camp Halleck were about changing for a southern station. This resulted in no serious inconvenience, as this escort, except for the very few days spent at rendezvous camps, were always divided into two, and often into as many as four parts. In the matter of the determination of the main astronomical stations, especially fruitful assistance was furnished on the part of the officers in charge of the United States Naval Observatory, the United States Lake Survey, and by the officers and certain operators of the Western Union Telegraph Company. I would particularly express my sense of obligation to Admiral Sands, of the United States Naval Observatory, whose active co operation secured to me the services of Professor J. R. Eastman at the observatory in Washington; to General C. B. Comstock, of the United States Lake Survey, who allowed Civilian Assistant O. B. Wheeler to perform similar service at the observatory at Detroit; to Mr. Orton, president, Messrs. Stager, Tinker, and Ladd, respectively, managers at Chicago, Washington, and San Francisco, of the Western Union Telegraph Company, as well as to Brigham Young, president of the Mormon Church, Salt Lake City, Utah, who, through the intervention of Hon. William H. Hooper, tendered the use of the Mormon telegraph from that point to Saint George, Utah. It requires but a hasty examination to conclude that the elements placed at my disposal were varied and complete, none too many, however, for the wants of an expedition to operate in so severe a section of country for such a length of time.

For the full co-operation of the supply departments of the Army too many thanks cannot be rendered. It would have been impossible, with the means placed at my disposal by the Engineer Department, to have conducted an expedition of such magnitude over so great a range of country within the limited time of one season, except for this very solid and generous assistance. It shall be among my endeavors to show that this has not been illy merited, and ask that reference be made to some of the succeeding pages for a hasty summary of most of the results that have been so far accomplished.

It is with the greatest difficulty that these can be made to seem not meager, since memory has to furnish so much material in the writing of this report, at a time when the majority of the notes are *en route*, or rather blockaded, upon the Union Pacific Railroad. To the many officers in command of military posts along our route, as well as quartermasters and commissaries, to very many gentlemen, superintendents of mines and residents of the mining districts, to various State, territorial, and county officials, to members of the public press, contiguous to areas of the exploration, and to various private citizens and others who have extended cordial aid and sympathy to the work allotted to my care, I desire to express my thanks, as well as those of several of the members of the expedition.

CHAPTER I.

The first principal rendezvous at Halleck Station, Nevada, on the Central Pacific Railroad, was established on the 3d of May, and the forces of the expedition were assembled entire within a few days, consisting, in addition to those already mentioned, as follows: Belonging to the engineer assistants and employés there were four topographers, one assistant surveyor, one assistant astronomical observer and computer, one chief geologist, one meteorologist, two collectors in natural history, one photographer, and guides, packers, laborers, &c., numbering thirty in all, which number was increased to thirty-one on the 1st of July by the addition of an assistant astronomical observer and assistant geologist; as quartermaster's employés, including chief packers, cargadores, guides, &c., fifteen. The transportation was as follows: One fifty-mule pack-train, one forty-mule pack-train, one instrument wagon, and two instrument-carts, two odometer vehicles, and riding-animals for officers, civilian assistants, and employés, as well as the escort. While waiting at Halleck Station, all the available time of the assistants was spent in journeys and examinations among the adjacent mountains within a radius from twelve to fourteen miles.

RENDEZVOUS CAMP NO. 1, AT HALLECK STATION, NEVADA, TO RENDEZVOUS CAMP NO. 2, NEAR BELMONT, NEVADA.

The entire expedition moved to Carlin, Nevada, at which point the first main astronomical station was to be established. A side party was here organized for work to the north and westward, and principally outside the zone traversed by the parties of the fortieth parallel survey. This party was to converge upon the remainder of main party No. 2, at Battle Mountain, Nevada, which had been sent there to establish a temporary camp at the commencement of that line. Main party No. 1 cut loose from the railroad about June 1, and passed to the southward, through Mineral Hill, Eureka, and Morey districts, to Belmont, about seven miles from which place the second rendezvous camp was established.

Two side topographical parties detoured from this line, coming in upon the main line successively at Eureka and Morey, visiting many mining districts and gaining valuable topographical and allied information. Main party No. 2, in charge of Acting Assistant Surgeon A. H. Cochrane, moving to the south, passed through Battle Mountain district, reaching Austin, as the first important point of any size. Side parties carried hasty examinations along the Toyabe Range and on either side of the Monitor Range.

The complete rendezvous near Belmont was accomplished on June 24. The field of operations thus far was entirely confined to Nevada.

RENDEZVOUS CAMP NO. 2, NEAR BELMONT, NEVADA, TO RENDEZVOUS CAMP NO. 3, AT CAMP INDEPENDENCE, CALIFORNIA.

The interval of time here included is a little more than thirty days. The examinations were over areas in both Nevada and California. Main party No. 2, in charge of Lieutenant Lyle, operated to the south and west, impinging with one side party constantly employed upon the very desert and little-known area to the south and southwest from Belmont, which is a portion of that large tract in Southwestern Nevada hitherto unexplored. I beg leave to append the report presented by this officer, marked Appendix B. Main party No. 1, with two side parties constantly engaged, moved to the south and east, reaching Pahranagat Valley for supplies prior to the direct march thence in nearly a due line toward Camp Independence, over one of the most desolate regions upon the face of the earth, and amid the scenes of disaster of those early emigrant trains who are accredited with having perished in "Death Valley." This entire section is known in common parlance among the settlers of the mining and mountain towns of Nevada as "Death Valley," while the "Death Valley proper" should be limited to that remarkable depression which, at its lowest surface, falls beneath the level of the ocean, and which lies principally in California.

It was thought at first that it would be impracticable to make this march with the entire train, and that it would be necessary to surround this desert section in traveling along lines partially known, and entering it at certain points with parties numbering not more than five or six. It was almost impossible to gain any accurate information of even the chances for grass and water from either white man or Indian, the erratic wanderings of the latter having scarcely reached a day's march from their own wick-e-ups. A party was dispatched to the southward, toward the Colorado, to establish a supply camp somewhere along Spring Mountain Range, upon which to converge, after the parties should have again crossed the "Death Valley," in their outward journey from Camp Independence. This arrangement proved most fortuitous. On the 23d of July, the rest of the main party were all together at Naquinta Springs, north and west from Tim-pah-ute Peak, with the desert stretching out along our western horizon. The objective point was a place since called Oasis Valley, known at the time to be sensibly to our westward, and containing good grass and water. This locality was reached after three days of the most severe marching, and was found to be a narrow valley, surrounded by low rolling mesas, from which broke, in many places, a large number of springs of good, clear water, but of varying thermal conditions. We remained here until joined by a messenger from Lieutenant Lyle's party, who reported still more terrible difficulties before us. This messenger came in accompanied by an Indian, and reported that he had left Lieutenant Lyle with a relief party on the eastern slope of the Inyo Range, and that he, in company with a guide by the name of Hahn, had gone forward to seek a camp to the eastward, and had been left far from this place by the guide, who apparently was confused from not knowing the country; this guide has never since been heard from. Lieutenant Lyle and party succeeded in reaching a little mining camp near Gold Mountain after great hardship. A subsequent guide sent by this officer explained that it would be impossible to send the main party immediately westward toward Camp Independence; consequently, after reaching Grape-vine Springs, which, at the western slope of the foot-hills of a range of this name, faces upon the northwestern arm of the main Death Valley, the train moved to the north and westward, to Deep Spring Valley, reaching there a road, while a party of picked men took up their route nearly due west to reach Camp Independence, no matter what the intervening obstacles, and succeeded in this after suffering what, up to that time, had been some of the most bitter experience that had ever fallen under my observation.

At this rendezvous, as in fact at all others, the time used for the recuperation of animals and arranging for supplies was economically employed by the professional force in local investigation and the preliminary reduction of notes.

At this point the expedition was joined by Lieutenant Lockwood.

RENDEZVOUS NO. 3, CAMP INDEPENDENCE, CALIFORNIA, TO NO. 4, AT COTTON-WOOD SPRINGS, NEVADA.

Lieutenant Lockwood, having been placed in charge of main party No. 2, was ordered to proceed well to the south, and then, turning to the eastward, to encircle several of the supposed interior and limited local basins, which, although lying in the natural profile which trends toward the Colorado, still are separate and inclosed. His party skirted the Sierras for a considerable distance below

Owen's Lake, and thence to the eastward and across the lower part of Death Valley. The general features of this trip, as well as those operations intrusted to his charge at subsequent times during the season, will appear in his preliminary report, herewith submitted and marked Appendix A. Besides a special party in charge of supplies, who sensibly followed the general direction of main line No. 2 toward the next rendezvous, another party followed an individual and separate line. Main party No. 1, in executive charge of Lieutenant Lyle, broke out of Owen's River Valley to the eastward at the head of Owen's Lake, and came to the mountains on the western side of Death Valley, where they were joined by a side party that had followed a line via the mines at Cerro Gordo, having struck this range of mountains higher up. The main camp was joined by myself after a very severe march, when it was found that a small party had gone to the northward to effect a connection between the two lines. A portion of this party returned, all, in fact, except Mr. Egan, the guide, who has never yet been heard from authentically; his fate, so far, is uncertain; that of any one to have followed him in the particular direction he was taking when last seen would have been *certain* death. More details of this matter occur in the report of Lieutenant Lyle.

The force was massed for the passage of Death Valley, and the camp in advance at Furnace Creek selected. The entrance to the valley was through a narrow, gorge-like cañon, presenting among its tortuous walls a variety of contour and color. The descent was very rapid, and the bed of the valley below, limited in horizon through the narrow opening by the far mountains to the eastward, met our eyes in strange and gloomy vibrations through the superheated atmosphere.

The cañon has been named after the valley, and photographic illustrations here made will give a far more tangible description than words can convey. Finally, one of the bugbears of the trip, that of crossing Death Valley, is over; this particular crossing was near the area of greatest depression, and Dr. Hoffman, with an assistant, was sent to the southward to take barometrical observations; he did not reach the point of greatest depression, however, but the observations from present rough calculations show a level below that of the sea. At our camp at Furnace Creek the thermometer at midnight recorded 109° F. This remarkable valley was crossed in four places.

The Amargosa Desert is next encountered, traversed, and camp made at its eastern edge. Here it became necessary to find the rendezvous that had been ordered to be established in the mountain range to the south and east, which result was determined only after much difficulty, owing partly to the surly nature of the Indians found here and the jaded condition of the men and animals of the command. Finally, intelligence was gotten through to the rendezvous, and their comparatively fresh animals did good service in bringing all the party to the camp, which had been selected at Cottonwood Springs, in a beautiful locality on the eastern slope of the Spring Mountain Range.

RENDEZVOUS NO. 4, COTTONWOOD SPRINGS, NEVADA, TO TRUXTON SPRINGS, ARIZONA TERRITORY, RENDEZVOUS CAMP NO. 5.

Prior to the establishing of the next rendezvous, the Colorado was to be crossed; a separate river party was to be organized and put in operation; the rendezvous itself was yet to be selected; also an escort from the Arizona side were to meet us at this point; the land forces were also to keep at work, up to their ordinary maximum capacity, and the plan for those operations, involving the points already mentioned as well as the seeming necessity of using the boats of the river party to cross the land forces at or near the foot of the Grand Cañon, had to be made up in advance, and with the knowledge that physical difficulties would prevent speedy communication in case of mishap. There was no small apprehension on my own part in regard to the success of the programme after it was made out. Subsequently, however, everything that was projected was accomplished, and at the appointed times.   The land parties were left in charge of Lieutenant Lockwood, still retaining their distinctive party organization, their first objective point being Saint George, in Southwestern Utah.   Their course to this point lay along three lines.   The party selected for the ascent of the Colorado reached Camp Mohave on the 11th of September, at which post the boats were stored.   The boats being in a somewhat damaged condition, several days were occupied in repairs and gathering supplies.

A guide was dispatched to meet the escort who were coming from Camp Hualapais as a re enforcement; these were to be directed to the rendezvous to be selected, and from thence the guide was to make his way to the northward, crossing the Colorado and reaching the main land camp; this he did with creditable ability and promptitude, and to his action alone belongs, in a measure, the success of the operations along this section.   The crossing at the foot of the Grand Cañon was reached on the morning of the 4th of October, and on the evening of the 5th the entire expedition was most successfully crossed.   One main line continued on directly to Truxton Springs; the remaining available force branched out in other directions.   Meanwhile the boat party entered the jaws of the Grand Cañon, not knowing what was before them.   Up to this time the rapids, though often very swift, had not been accompanied with heavy falls, and the estimate for the time requisite to reach the mouth of the Diamond Creek, (called "Diamond River" by Ives,) or the most desirable point at which to connect with the land camp, was based on our experience up to that time, with supposed due allowance for increasing difficulties, and so arranged in the instructions given to the relief parties.

Subsequent revelations showed how inadequate was this plan, and also the chances for suffering that may arise from want of careful judgment and forethought.   However, on the 19th of October, after many difficulties, in comparison with which any other of the hardships and privations of the expedition sink into insignificance, the exhausted boat party reached the mouth of Diamond Creek, and are next day gladdened by the sight of the relief party, who visited this point the second time to their assistance.   This river trip, occupying only thirty-three days, was quite an exploration of itself, and will be given its due prominence in the final report.

The Mohave Indians accompanying us on this trip proved to be of invaluable assistance, and although several times wishing to desert, because of the tedious labor and their fear of the Pah-Utes, with whom they were at war, nevertheless proved faithful and industrious to the end.

A side party succeeded in reaching the head of the Diamond Creek after some difficult climbing.

The complete rendezvous at Truxton Springs was accomplished on the 23d of October.

FROM RENDEZVOUS NO. 5 TO RENDEZVOUS NO. 6, PRESCOTT, ARRIZONA TERRITORY.

The main line with the heavy train debouched to the southward, reaching the military road from Camp Mohave to Prescott, and then pushed on in advance to establish the camp.   Main party No. 2 followed the rim of the watershed, dividing the waters that approach the Colorado direct and along the Grand Cañon, and those flowing toward tributaries that, joining, enter farther to the southward.

Lieutenant Lyle, with a picked escort, broke to the south and east, with Camp Date Creek as an objective point, and thence via Bradshaw mines to Prescott.   Another side party visited the Hualapais district, detoured thence in its march to the southward, coming into the military road near Camp Hualapais, while still another party, going as far as Mohave, brought instruments, supplies, and data deposited there, hence to Prescott.   The rendezvous at Prescott was completed November 6.   Winter was coming on, and being at least three weeks late in reaching this locality, it was determined to diminish slightly the size of the expedition—which had at all times been too large—at this point; carrying out this plan, the fearful sequel determined that three who had left us were among those unfortunates in the late Wickenburgh stage massacre, another one of the atrocities committed, so far as circumstantial evidence can determine, at the hands of the Indians fed and fostered by our Government upon reservations.

RENDEZVOUS CAMP NO. 6 TO RENDEZVOUS NO. 7, AT CAMP APACHE, ARIZONA TERRITORY.

The force, fairly organized, started out well in hand. · Party No. 1 moving to the eastward across the Verde River at the caves, about thirty miles north of Camp Verde, thence in a nearly due straight line reaching the high mesa, and finally the northern end of San Francisco Mountains, about which detailed examinations were made, thence turning to the south and east. Camp Apache was an objective point, and the divide of the waters between the basin of the Little Colorado and those of the Verde and Salt Rivers was sensibly the line followed. We were troubled with some snow, and now and then unpleasant winds, all of which was agreeably modified after breaking from the mesa down into the Tonto Basin. The distance proved to be greater than was anticipated, and men and animals reached Apache much jaded.

Main party No. 2 had arrived at this same point a day or two previous, having crossed our line, reaching the Little Colorado, thence via head of the White Mountains. Only a short time was spent here, as, already so long in the field, nearly every one was threadbare and ready for rest.

A photograph of the White Mountain Apaches on ration day was secured.

RENDEZVOUS NO. 7, TO FINAL RENDEZVOUS CAMP NO. 8, AT CAMP LOWELL, TUCSON, ARIZONA TERRITORY.

The march between these points was conducted simply in two main lines, one via San Carlos River and Camp Grant, the second via Pinal Mountains and Florence, on the Gila River.

Tucson was reached on the evening of the 5th of December, and preparations for disbanding already begun were hastened to a conclusion, and on the 11th everything had been disposed of and those of the parties who were to go either to San Francisco or Washington had departed. Seventy-one remaining mules, the property of the quartermaster's department, were turned over to the depot quartermaster, and forty-seven others, engineer property, were sold, with a view of being used as transportation in the coming campaign, and it is hoped that these, as also the several experienced packers, who remained, may be doing good service in the fight against the Apaches in the war, supposed already to have been commenced by General Crook, commanding the department.

Thus, in the windings in and out of the main and various detached parties a reconnaissance line of 6,327 miles has been traversed, or nearly twice the shortest distance from Washington to San Francisco. A little more than 83,000 square miles of territory has been examined, lying in the following-named political divisions: Nevada, 32,000; California, 19,000; Utah, 1,200; Arizona, 31,000. It is safe to say that five-eighths of this is new ground. The expense has been a little less than $1 per square mile; per square acre not to exceed sixteen one-hundredths cents.

The result has exceeded my most sanguine expectations, so much so that present experience would compel me to ask for two seasons to cover a similar-sized area, and it is hoped will contribute data worthy a place among the records of the Department in regard to this portion of our territory. The line has crossed the route of two railroads already projected, the Atlantic and Pacific, and Texas Pacific, along areas that will have to be traversed by the Utah Southern, and affords the requisite information for those routes north and south which are so much needed in the development of the mining interest, and which will be eventually required to hold together the diverse interests of sections separated by large distances latitudinally.

It may be said that much of this ground has been visited before, but, although the first party of recorded explorers, who visited sections familiar among the annals of this trip as early as 1540, more than three centuries ago, and have been succeeded by various parties subsequently up to the present time, still the operations of this season have but joined on to, elaborated upon, and to a certain extent completed their work, mapping sensibly only those portions hitherto known as unexplored instrumentally upon the able map of the Western States and Territories compiled in the Engineer Department by General G. K. Warren, at that time lieutenant in the Corps of Topographical Engineers.

CHAPTER II.

I shall endeavor in this chapter to give the general results upon the subjects mentioned in the letter of instructions from the Chief of Engineers; and, with this in view, shall divide them into heads, as follows: 1st, astronomical; 2d, topographical; 3d, physico-geographical; 4th, meteorological; 5th, geological; 6th, department of natural history, &c.

ASTRONOMICAL.

The great want in the mapping of the western portion of our territory has been the accurate establishment of astronomical positions. The plan adopted this season has been to secure, at the most proper and available intervals of the perimeter of the area surveyed, the main astronomical stations. During this season these have been to a certain extent accessory to, and governed by, the movements of the parties of the expedition. The locations are as follows: Carlin and Battle Mountain, Nevada, on Central Pacific Railroad, Austin, Nevada; Camp Independence, California; Saint George, Utah; and Prescott, Arizona Territory. Including those determined in 1869, there have been established for main stations, under my supervision, eleven points, in the interior of our western territory. In nine of these cases, the longitude has been determined by telegraph. All have been solidly marked with stone monuments, and are available for future reference.

The principal observer, Mr. E. P. Austin, presents a hasty report, submitted herewith, and marked Appendix C, giving a general notion of the character of the work, and the prospective value of the results. Another of the observers, Mr. Marvine, who also at times has had his attention directed to matters of geology, could, if present during the time of arranging the material for a preliminary report, bear more particular testimony regarding the results at Saint George, Utah, and at Prescott, Arizona Territory. His observations, however, when reduced by the computer, will be presented in proper form in the final report.

In order to comprehend fully the character of the value of this astronomical work, the full report will give, in addition to the reductions of our own observers, those of Messrs. Eastman and Wheeler, respectively, of the United States Naval Observatory, at Washington, and that of the United States Lake Survey, at Detroit.

At the intermediate astronomical stations, the observations have been taken with sextants giving a check more particularly upon the latitudes.

The majority of the stations were confined to the two main lines of the survey, and the character of the work varies in no remarkable particular from that ordinarily performed in the Pacific Railroad surveys. Data from these observations will be properly grouped in tables for future reference.

TOPOGRAPHICAL.

The plan pursued has been to attach one topographer to each of the main and side parties, who was assisted by one observer taking odometer readings, and another person to read the barometer for relative and absolute altitude of the station.

In the frame-work of the map are the main astronomical points, the intermediate astronomical points coming in at the ends of the daily marches, while between each two of these latter the topographer takes as many stations as may be needed to satisfy him in regard to the details.

The base line is then the meandered line, measured by the odometer, checked by astronomical positions and angular bearings from prominent mountain peaks.

The portable transits employed, having a telescope of considerable focal power, give quite accurate readings for the bearings, and a skillful topographer, after a little practice, varies but slightly in his latitudes and departures from those given by the astronomical positions. The aneroid readings give data for a general profile of the routes and the heights of the stations, and after these observations are reduced by comparing with the cistern barometer, give a series of results of surprising relative accuracy.

In the vicinity of the rendezvous camps more time was available, and more minute surveys carried out. The contours of the areas, covered by mineral development in two mining districts, were taken.

The method of moving in two lines, flanked at least by one side party adjacent to each, has worked very successfully, and in a great measure accounts for the very extensive results obtained topographically. The difficulty of keeping these parties supplied, and in a state of active co-operation, calls for very constant, strenuous exertions, however, on the part of the officer in charge.

As a certain allotment of funds and material had been made for one season's work to cover a certain area, it became necessary, in order to consummate the results expected, to work with much celerity and little or no intermission, and the force at my disposal were constantly pressed with labors that gave them little if any rest, and no recreation from the commencement to the end of the season. It is with no little satisfaction that I can bear testimony to the willingness of the civilian assistants and employés, with scarce an exception, to make any and all exertions, or undergo such privations as were required of them.

In gaining topographical information, special attention was given to the determination of the perimeter line of the watersheds of the exterior and interior basins; to the relative portions of mountain and valley; to the size and extent of the arable, mineral, and desert sections; of the distribution of springs, streams, timber, &c., all of which are to appear in the final map or maps.

The areas inhabited by the Indian tribes are also to be marked out, and the varieties of observations afford material for the construction of a number of maps.

The possible location for routes by rail, or common roads, along lines sensibly north and south, have been carefully studied, and to this end the expedition has followed out and made use of the system employed in the earlier surveys for a railroad route from the Mississippi to the Pacific Ocean; more accuracy having been obtained because of the superior character of the astronomical stations, and the improvement in field instruments now used.

The large field traversed while upon various trips since 1868, up to that of the present season, has rendered me conversant with a considerable section of country over which, in the final topographical map, a more systematic nomenclature can be adopted.

Among those portions prosecuted more in detail, and presenting novel and interesting results is the survey of the Colorado, partly hydrographic in its nature, and which adds unique information to the topographical knowledge of our continent.

The general tendency of projecting too much has been felt in this undertaking, and must always follow as the experience of any one who estimates for a scheme of exploration, no matter how little or how greatly elaborate among those sections of our western territory still unmapped, where the physical obstacles are so varied and difficult.

PHYSICO-GEOGRAPHICAL.

The operations of the past season have been conducted in a great measure in and around the Great American Desert.

Go where you will in your journey westward, from the Rocky Mountains to the Pacific Ocean, you must cross its barren and uninviting plains, valleys, or mountains.   Its configuration is varied, as are many of its local characteristics; in width ranging from seventy-five to two hundred and fifty miles, but nowhere narrowing so that an east and west line can be prolonged entirely through arable sections.

The elevations of this great area vary, from the depression in Death Valley, below the level of the sea, to mountain valleys, from six to seven thousand feet in altitude, surrounded by rugged and often desolate ranges, whose summits tower to heights of eleven and twelve thousand feet.

The general trend of these mountain chains from the fortieth to the thirty-fifth parallel is sensibly north and south, with spurs and ridges that bear for the general part to the northwest and southeast, the eastern slopes of the main ridges being by far the most gentle.

Passing into Arizona, the continuity of the characteristic trend of the Cordillera system is somewhat broken in that area occupying so large a portion of Northeastern Arizona, that will be named upon the maps as the Colorado Plateau.   Upon the summit of this grand plateau one encounters the rolling and broken mesa formation through which have obtruded at many points volcanic mountain peaks, that lift their black sides far in the horizon.

Through the middle of the Territory the ranges, formed of the more primitive rocks, steer on in their course, and are met, as it were, by other ranges that, converging in direction, follow onward in their deliberate advance, massing in the Sierra Madres of Mexico.

The present map submitted will give somewhat of a general view of these more prominent features.

Physical geography details, always having more direct reference to the vertical lines of a survey, have been sought after, and the wants of the case attended to so far as possible.   The positive and relative altitudes of a multitude of points have been secured.

Profiles along many lines of the basins, both exterior and interior, can be produced; the configurations of the mountains, valleys, rivers, creeks, and springs, in their general relation, have been noted.   The character and supposed extent of the great Colorado Plateau, the peculiar features of which have, for the first time, been delineated, were partially studied and need but one more expedition to complete.

Examinations while ascending the famous cañon of the Colorado chronicle, *in memoriam*, additions to those data, gradually being collated, referring to the beginning of the creation of the world; and while watching the gloomy sides of these grand walls, listening to the confused mutterings of the restless waters, whose continual flow through geologic years have so seldom awakened a sound beyond their own echoes, comes the thought that the time necessary for the creation, full development, and extinction of one single animal race, falls into insignificance in comparison with the eras that may have passed while this erosive agent of nature was stealing slowly down to its present bed.

The exploration has determined the existence and limits of several basins, completely inclosed, without drainage to the ocean and outside either of the Great Salt Lake or Humboldt Basins, principally found in Nevada, to the east of the Sierras and north of latitude 35° 30′; of these the Death Valley Basin is characteristic.

The face of the country, especially in those locations where the primitive rocks are superimposed unconformably, by volcanic material belonging to the older series, is rapidly changing by denudations; the constant action of these degradations being to decrease the declivities of the mountains, carrying the *débris* far out into the valleys, the disintegration constantly furnishing earthy material for new series of plants from age to age.

Along very many areas in Nevada and Arizona quite extensive forests fringe the high mountains and plateaus. The grand Colorado Plateau, so immense in size, is, over a great share of its surface, covered with pine forests and parks.

The greater portion of the area examined in Southeastern California was of the most barren and desolate nature, the bare and brown rocks seldom being relieved by any sort of vegetation.

Piñon pine and a stunted growth of mountain cedar abound in frequent localities in Nevada. The pine found after crossing the Colorado is similar in character to what is known as the short-leaved southern pine. Fir and hemlock are noted along the slopes of the high mountains; mesquite, mountain mahogany, and cactus in the valleys.

The view from Humphrey's Peak, on the San Francisco Mountains, is along a magnificent and extended horizon to the northeast, east, and southeast, limited by the plateau formation with its mesa bluffs of various colors, on the west by the ranges along the Colorado, and on the south and southwest by the Black Hills and Mazatzal, while in this direction, also, the grand peaks of the White Mountain Range tower in the horizon. At our feet lay the upturned mouths of numerous craters, upon the sides of which, in many cases, heavy timber is growing, undisturbed by those volcanic bursts which, in their efforts to reach an equilibrium, carried high in air the ground now under our feet, and raised that lofty pile upon which we were standing, which served a long time as a vent for those interior fires, and then became forever silent, leaving what we now see—the bed of an immense extinct crater.

It will be with the greatest interest that the future observer carries his studies among the lofty peaks, the broken mesas, and astonishing cañons of this great Colorado Plateau, which in its geographical area covers spaces aggregating, possibly, 60,000 square miles, and distributed in four political divisions, viz: Utah, Arizona, New Mexico, and Colorado.

METEOROLOGICAL.

These observations comprise the usual full series, taken with the latest and most improved instruments.

At the rendezvous camps hourly observations were taken for the purpose of computing approximate tables of the horary corrections at various altitudes through the mountain regions. In addition, frequent observations for the correction of the aneroids and with a view to obtaining a reference scale.

At all camps the usual tri-daily barometric, &c., observations were taken, while at each one of the minor topographical stations the aneroid barometer was read.

The two hospital stewards who were the observers assisted at the hourly stations. The computations are now being made, and the results will appear in sheets giving the general meteorological record, the comparisons of the aneroids and the hourly series, with plottings of the approximate horary curves.

The results of this season, comprised with those of 1869, add considerably to the meteorological data of this region. The working-up of these results is at present in the hands of Lieutenant Lockwood, and, proving favorable as now expected, will contribute a little to the want that can only be supplied by establishing a comprehensive system of permanent meteorological stations, (for minute and careful observations,) at high altitudes, throughout the entire western interior.

GEOLOGICAL.

Investigations in this department were committed to the care of G. K. Gilbert, who was assisted a portion of the time by A. R. Marvine, after the completion of astronomical work at Saint George, Utah, and at desultory intervals by C. A. Ogden.

I shall present herewith, marked Appendix D, the report of Mr. Gilbert, which will speak for itself, and sustains the high character entertained regarding his labors and abilities. Mr. Marvine is at present engaged in placing the results of his examinations in the form of a report.

NATURAL HISTORY.

Dr. Walter J. Hoffman, in charge, was assisted by two collectors, besides the volunteer aid of certain other members of the expedition, to whom credit will be given in due time.

The collections of coleoptera and botanical specimens have been large and comprehensive; in many other branches the scarcity of the material and rapidity of the movements prevented more complete and careful collections.

By authority of the Engineer Department, and through the kindness of Professor S. F. Baird, these collections will be at once sent to the Smithsonian Institution, under whose directions the examination of specimens will be conducted.

MINERALOGY.

This department has been in the hands of Dr. Walter J. Hoffman, while various members have contributed silver-ore specimens. A report on this subject is being compiled by this gentleman.

In this connection let me say that an attempt is being made to gather a very large collection, fully representing the silver ores of the Pacific coast, by large and characteristic specimens, collected in duplicate, and deposited in the national museums of the Smithsonian and West Point. The nucleus already collected gives promise of good results.

MAGNETIC OBSERVATIONS.

There have been observations for declination and dip; for the former a field theodolite, simply, was used; for the latter a dip circle, procured from the United States Coast Survey, which was, however, lost in the Grand Cañon of the Colorado, among many other very valuable and useful articles. The record of the observations up to this time was preserved.

PHOTOGRAPHS.

In the hands of Mr. O'Sullivan, well known in connection with his labors on the Fortieth Parallel Survey and Darien Expedition, a little less than three hundred negatives have been produced, illustrating the general appearance of the country, the mining districts, certain geological views, and a full and characteristic representation of that very grand and peculiar scenery, found only among the cañons of the Colorado; a more unique series has hardly been produced in this country.

To add more testimony illustrative of the character and general appearance of the areas traversed, various sketches have been made along the line of the routes, and among the cañons of the Colorado.

MEANS OF COMMUNICATION.

The close of the present century bids fair to be the era, above all others, of increased rail communication. The great necessity for, and interest evinced in, pushing routes through to the Pacific has been accomplished; one line is complete; three others are projected, and will, without doubt, be built. The east and west lines, then, are secured. Now, it seems that north and south lines are needed to communicate with these east and west lines, to be adjuncts to their usefulness in the tendency to develop the mineral resources of this portion of our territory.

There should be three roads running south from the Central Pacific Railroad and between the Sierras and Wahsatch Mountains, situated as follows:

The first, already projected, bears southerly from Salt Lake to the Colorado River, to cross near the foot of the Grand Cañon.

The second to leave the railroad, pass through Washoe, and thence along immediately east of the Sierras.

A third leaving the railroad in a central position, and crossing the Colorado River at the mouth of the Virgin. Let these be narrow-gauge roads if you will, but the country needs them to carry supplies and material to its mines, and to bring ore and bullion from them.

From the reports of Messrs. Lockwood and Lyle, I am led to believe that a new mail and wagon route may be constructed from Saint George, Utah, to Prescott, Arizona Territory. Granting this, it could at the present time be occupied as a mail-route, and upon building the wagon-road, troops could then be moved from north to south in our western interior without the heavy expense of first transporting them to the seaboard. This route will be through Salt Lake City, on a stage-road to Saint George, thence, by a road to be constructed at little expense, to Prescott, Arizona Territory.

In the future, and after the proper development of the mines that have been and are still being discovered in the vicinity of the Colorado River, the means of communication on this river will be both increased and strengthened.

This exploration has determined that navigation in suitable crafts can be carried much higher than has been supposed. A little healthy competition, in case there was traffic enough to warrant it, would soon lessen the prices from San Francisco to Mohave from $80 per ton, at present demanded, as I understand, from the citizens.

However, I am pleased to learn that the present navigation company are offering liberal inducements to parties desiring to ship ores by their route, on the return trip to San Francisco.

Steamers at present navigate as high as Camp Mohave, four hundred and twenty-five miles from the mouth of the river; they have often carried cargoes to El Dorado Cañon, fifty-nine miles higher. One steamer succeeded in reaching Callville, about ninety-five miles from Mohave, without material difficulty. It is concluded, should the necessity present itself, that navigation by steam-power may be carried to the foot of the Grand Cañon, or fifty-seven miles beyond Callville. The relation of the power of the engine to the size and draught of the steamer should be changed for navigating above Mohave, increasing motive-power and decreasing draught and size. Possibly the barges should be decreased in tonnage from one hundred and fifty to one hundred tons. Each steamer should be fitted with a steam-capstan, and at certain points ring-bolts should be fastened in the rocks above the heads of the rapids, for cordelling purposes.

I would like especially to mention my indebtedness to Captain J. A. Mellon, of the steamer Cocopah, for certain sensible information on this subject.

Let us suppose that we can navigate as far as the foot of the Grand Cañon; the question naturally comes up, what necessity, present or prospective, calls for this? I will answer, so far as my observation leads to a conclusion, that the wants of the present century will ask for no line of transportation to ascend the river higher than Cottonwood Island, which point might be made the depot for traffic to interior mining localities in Nevada and Arizona; (see map.)

But to return to the east and west lines, now in process of construction; it seems certain, from the increased evidence adduced, from the nature of the travel and transportation along that single line already constructed, that the time is not greatly in the future that, if we expect to gather transcontinental shipments, some one road, reliable at all seasons of the year, must be completed:

and the experience which my present travels has afforded pledges opinion in favor of the line lately surveyed in the vicinity of the thirty-fifth parallel.

INDIANS.

The experience of this season has given considerable further opportunity for studying the Indian character, their habits of life, geographical distribution, &c. This experience has in no way produced a sympathy with that class of well-intentioned but illy-informed citizens who claim that the Indians are a much-abused race.

My several trips of the past four years have allowed full opportunity for immediate observation on this subject; therefore, in a subsequent report, I propose to present my views at greater length.

The areas inhabited by, and known as the country of, the Shoshones, Pah-Utes, Chemehuevis, Utes, Mohaves, Seviches, Hualapais, Apache-Mohaves, Cosninas, Apache, (Tontos, Pinals, Coyoteros and Arivapas,) &c., have been pretty accurately determined, and will be mapped out. It was with no little surprise that, upon examining the best sources of information, viz, that obtained through Army officers, it was found that the actual number of the Apache warriors, who could take the field, would not exceed fifteen hundred. Major John Green, of the First United States Cavalry, who has had considerable experience among them, positively asserted that they could not muster twelve hundred men from all the tribes, including the White Mountain Indians, many of whom have been upon reservations since 1868.

All the tribes, without exception, belong to that wild, roving breed known as "Mountain Indians." Their lawless and migratory life has carried them beyond the notion of anything like order, even among their own people.

It may not be uninteresting, at this particular period, when there are so many diverse opinions, or rather theories, extant regarding the position or supposed condition of the hostile Indians in the Southwest, to acquaint the War Department, through the medium of this report, with the influence that the Indians, as we found them, have had as a help or as a hinderance to the objects of this exploration, so that at subsequent periods, when other parties shall have in hand the duties of surveying out remote, inaccessible, and inhospitable regions, they may have the benefit of the experience.

The general plan of moving in two lines, and receiving the co-operation of small side parties, cannot but work admirably in any scheme of geographical exploration. Let us see how much friendly Indians can be of service.

We will premise that it is incompatible to divide up into four or five parties in a hostile country without calling on the military posts for greater escorts than could be reasonably expected from them; therefore, as in the present case, it was found necessary to move in two parties only, while engaged in those parts of Arizona known as the habitation of the hostile Apache. This fact explains the principal hinderance. It is almost impossible to obtain white guides who have any accurate knowledge of regions sensibly new, while hardly any nook or corner can be found not well known to the Indian; hence in the selection of suitable camping-places, and as assistants to a natural guide, or to a white man who shall exercise judgment as to the movements of the command, their services can be made very valuable. The entire expedition, composed of officers, soldiers, and civilians averaged from eighty to one hundred and ten, being divided into parties varying from five to fifty.

The little parties are really the ones that accomplish the most actual work. In Nevada, to each one of these little parties an Indian could be attached, and oftentimes two, who, in view of a small remuneration and plenty of food, served both as guide and laborer, thereby causing a positive benefit, and, in all cases, relieving that apprehension of danger which all parties in a new country must experience, and which, to many, is more uncomfortable than danger itself.

From among the Pah-Utes, in the Spring Mountain Range, often as many as seven or eight guides and messengers were employed at one time. These Indians have been considered friendly for some years, but frequently prospectors, in parties of two, going out into the mountains, never return. They have, however, a wonderful regard for a superior force.

The semi-hostile Indians, as the Seviches, south of the Colorado, and the renegade Hualapais, found bordering the country of the Apache-Mohaves, can be made useful to a certain extent by a party of respectable size. No squad less than five in number should at present trust themselves among them.

From the friendly Indians the ranchmen and miners get more or less assistance in and around their farms, working in the mines and as messengers; in this way they greatly facilitate the early development in this section.

Now, how is all this changed, when one comes into the hostile Apache country! A party with a proper guard may travel for weeks and never see an Indian, except here and there, outside of range, and then generally more wild than a deer.

In conducting examinations, a single member even of the professional corps must be provided with a guard before it is safe for him to pass the brow of a hill in front of camp.

By dint of great perseverance, a semi-friendly Indian may be impressed into the service of guiding a party into a hostile country, but there is no certainty that he will be true to his trust.

This hasty sketch gives some notion of the disadvantages of conducting an exploration over a country occupied by hostile Indians; the subject needs only to be suggested to call attention to the fact that every essential detail is, of a necessity, greatly contracted.

The well-beaten Apache trails from Arizona to Sonora attest the fact of the lines long followed in raids upon the Mexican ranches and stock.

The legend exists among the Apaches that they were once a concentrated and powerful race, far surpassing in strength the Navajoes, with whom they had frequent encounters. Their horses, cattle, and sheep were plenty; their crops large; their chiefs came from a line of hereditary princes. Finally, dissensions arising, the cupidity of certain upstart chieftains caused troublous times, the dividing into separate bands, and a general war among themselves resulting. The end came in complete desolation and poverty. This continued nearly up to the time of the acquisition of the territory by the United States, when, against a common enemy, the white man, they banded together for defense. The secret of their great terror to the whites is their lawless and roving life, giving celerity to their movements, with great powers of endurance. The common experience in settling questions with such tribes, and the only one that has proven successful, is to thoroughly whip them, after which they never make any determined resistance.

The Indians of Arizona have never been made to feel that they had any master beyond their own will for a wild and Bohemian life. No continuous concentration of force has been directed to their rancherias and villages, there to meet and teach them that they must give up their habits of violence and murder, or submit to the inevitable fate of destruction.

Let the Indian policy of this Government be what it may, the Indian question in Arizona will never be settled until the campaigns of an energetic officer shall thoroughly whip and subdue them. Let this be done, and they are then as amenable as the Shoshones of Nevada or the Hualapais of Northwestern Arizona.

The tribes encountered during the present season will be denominated, respectively, as friendly, semi-friendly, and hostile. In the first we must place the Shoshones, Pah-Utes, Chemehuevis, Utes,

Mohaves, and possibly the Hualapais, as they are now nearly all on a reservation, and no longer consider it policy to hold out against the whites. In the second, Seviches, Apache-Mohaves, Cosninas, and Apache-Coyoteros. Among those undoubtedly hostile are the Apaches, known as Tontos, Pinals, and Arivapas. Other Apache tribes, as the Mescaleros, Bonitos, and those governed by Cachise, were outside the limits embraced in the present exploration.

In this connection it seems almost impossible not to revert to that source of disaster to three members of the expedition, who were victims in the Wickenburgh stage massacre, for which I most thoroughly believe the Indians are responsible. Considerable trouble was taken in investigating this case through the agency of parties sent to the locality, and the weight of evidence convicts the Indians, and possibly those, too, who were drawing their food and supplies from the Government. From a careful study of the case, I am led to believe that the Indians in the vicinity of the Date Creek reservation, as in fact those in various other localities in Arizona, gathered courage from the fact that a peace commissioner had lately been in their midst, and hence thought with the greater impunity to commit this deed of violence with which their innate character had so much natural sympathy. Here were three men who had mastered all the toils and hardships of a severe campaign, who started homeward pleased with the thought of dangers escaped and duties well performed, who, after passing what was supposed to be unsafe ground, fell victims to an Indian ambuscade. One of these, a young man just entering upon his career, with years of promise before him, one drop of whose blood the whole Apache race could not expiate, parted with his life; and forgetting all else, in the records of humanity, this life, as well as that of the others, should be charged to the Indians.

Wherever opportunity afforded, conciliatory talks were held with the Indians, and the result was advantageous in the case of the Pah-Utes and Mohaves. The former tribe, assisted by the Chemehuevis, who are an allied race, had been at war for five years with the Mohaves; the cause of this difficulty was sought out, advice given, and during the river trip the captain of the Mohaves, who accompanied us, had a meeting with one of the Pah-Ute captains, through whom an amicable adjustment was arranged.

The ruins of the famous Aztec tribes, a name so rhythmical in legend, were met in many localities. Their status can be referred to as little better than—if indeed quite as good as—those Pueblo Indians, among whom we now have evidences remaining in the Zunis and Moquis besides other local tribes on the Rio Grande, however great their numbers might have been. They were doubtless driven from their accustomed habitations by the Apaches coming from the southward, and forced to seek for shelter those caves occupied by them as fortifications, finally becoming extinct, as must every race in the presence and in the line of progress of that race superior both in numbers and intelligence.

SITES FOR MILITARY POSTS.

These refer to positions for occupation and for operations. The selection for the sites of temporary or permanent military posts generally originates with the general commanding either the division or department, and their basis is determined by his peculiar ideas of the necessity therefor.

Scouting parties ordinarily discover a sufficient number of places, in advance of the pushing forward of troops into a new, hostile Indian country, and their reports go on record at the headquarters; therefore the results on this subject will be shown simply in marking upon the final map those points that can be conveniently occupied for military posts or scouting camps.

INFLUENCE OF CLIMATE.

The climatology of the Pacific coast, although a subject of great importance and interest, yet, for the want of systematic data, remains in a very vague condition.

So far as the climatic oscillations now in progress are concerned, the general observations of so hasty an exploration can bear no great testimony. Beyond the geological examinations that notice the translation of alluvial material by direct atmospheric influences, our investigations were confined more directly to the quite complete series of meteorological observations. At the present time these are not in shape to be analyzed.

The principal portion of our time was spent in the great basin of the Colorado, and among some of the outlying or rather interior basins to the northwest. At present, throughout this area, arable sections are scarce, and but few of these have been entered by the settlers. Little by little, however, the desert edges will be reclaimed by irrigation, and reference has only to be made to that narrow strip of mountain valleys in the western portion of Utah, now inhabited by the Mormons, to show what the hand of industry and necessity may do in reclaiming arid lands and bringing them under cultivation. I cannot but believe that many of the mountain valleys in Nevada and Arizona will at no distant date become peopled, as are now many of those from Salt Lake to the southward.

It is generally admitted that large amounts of the aqueous vapors from the oceans rise to the higher currents of the atmosphere and are there carried, by rapid rates of motion, through long and wide intervals. The great atmospheric gulf stream of the middle and southwestern Pacific Ocean impinges with its humid strata along the entire Pacific coast. A portion in the higher currents, from local surroundings, reaches its maximum of condensation while passing over the coast range, while the remainder progresses onward until it is caught by the Sierras, where it deposits in the form of rain or snow.

The upper portion of the great interior basin beyond lies exterior to this influence. The broad Tulare Valley of California in between the Sierras and the coast, if it could rise up and catch this moisture, would become the scene of a luxuriant vegetation, whereas now the changes from the very wet to the very dry season, annually, are strongly marked.

Let us suppose, however, that from the irrigating power that can be secured from the streams that rise in the Sierras, and have their primal source from these same humid currents of the upper air, 5,000,000 of acres could be brought under cultivation, with fields of corn and wheat, groves of fruit and forest trees, and varieties of vegetation, will it not be reasonable to conclude that, during this interval, the local surrounding climate will undergo slow changes, so that the atmosphere charged with humidity from this immense evaporation will bring about its own deposits of rain, thereby causing a temporary vacuum, as it were, into which would fall portions of the moisture, at that time in passage in the higher regions? Such a theory is not yet supported by known and pronounced facts; it may not be uninteresting to consider it in advance as among those changes to climate that the industries of man are producing. This same surcharged upper stratum that strikes the coast farther to the southward, follows the bed of the Colorado for a long distance, and the effects from it branch farther out as the approach is made to the higher ranges of mountains, situated in the northeastern portion of that basin.

In this direction, the Sierras having lost their specific character, and breaking over toward the coast range, do not impose a barrier, and none is met until the Wahsatch and Uintah Mountains are reached, in whose higher altitudes it is understood that the humidity, that has had its origin at the surface of the sea, is felt, and can be noticed by the more delicate meteorological instruments.

Extreme ranges of temperature have been encountered along the route, ranging from 8° F. as the maximum cold, to 109° F. at midnight, for the greatest heat. Difference of wet and dry bulb readings, give a range from 5° F. to 45° F. The equability of temperature and regularity of the winds and rains of most of the valleys south of 38° latitude and until Southern Arizona is reached, combine to render the climate a very healthy and agreeable one.

AGRICULTURAL AND GRAZING LANDS.

As before stated, the arable lands of Nevada are very small in relative amount; contrasting Nevada with Arizona, the latter has the advantage in relative proportions, as will be shown by the statistical map to be constructed.

Nevada cannot claim to be an agricultural section, but most of the local wants for the mining inhabitants could be supplied from home production. In Arizona, in and around Prescott, along the valley of the upper Gila, Salt and Verde Rivers, south of Tucson, along the Santa Cruz River and Sonoita Creek, there is an area capable of sustaining quite an agricultural population; some of the finest soil that I have ever seen has lately been broken up along the Gila, and around the settlement called Florence.

In the matter of natural facilities for grazing large herds of stock, Arizona ranks Nevada; in the number of mining districts Nevada leads far in the advance. As far as the probable amount of bullion from the two, at a time twenty years from now, is concerned, it is hard to say. It is believed that after the Indian difficulty is settled, and railroads are brought into Arizona, that districts already examined will be worked profitably, and stimulus given to further and more careful prospecting. When the Indians have become peaceable, the valleys and rolling foot-hills will afford the most excellent pasturage for very large herds of stock, with their covering of bunch and gramma grasses. At the present time, stock not herded by a respectable force is not safe in any portion of Arizona, except at certain localities along the Lower Gila and Colorado, and in the Hualapais country, or northwestern part of the Territory.

It is safe, also, to say that the time is close at hand when these areas will become great grazing-grounds, for, in the onward march of population, the stock-ranches skirting the tributaries to the west of the Mississippi and Missouri Rivers must give way to the settler who wishes to till the soil, and the value per acre gradually gets beyond where it becomes profitable to use it for stock-raising purposes. Thus, year by year, droves of horses, cattle, and sheep are being driven more and more toward the far West; valleys in Nevada that in 1869 were uninhabited were heard to have been filled up subsequently with stock during the interval, and within two years every available stock-range in the State will have been appropriated.

Very little game is found in and around the more desert portions of Nevada and Arizona; in fact it may be said that there is a zone of comparatively no game, whether large or small, limited on the west by the Sierras, on the east by the Wahsatch Mountains, north by 40°, and south by 35° 30' north latitude.

In Northeastern and Eastern Arizona many herds of deer and antelope were seen; bear, of the brown or cinnamon and grizzly varieties, and wild turkey. A certain strip, commencing on the eastern part and continuing south into Arizona, is also frequented by many species of game.

Coal, of economic value, lay but at one portion of our route, so far as had been discovered, and that was at the northwestern end of the White Mountains. Many carboniferous strata appear, but the coal-beds are wanting.

In and around Death Valley, among the cañons of the Colorado, and at very many mining districts, granite and various volcanic rocks, offering a good variety of building material, were noted.

MINES.

This subject, which above all others merits the most attention of any one of the practical and immediately remunerative interests belonging to the field of this exploration, had not a prominent place in the letter of instructions. However, my experience on the western slope at other times than during the present season has thrown me much among the mines and miners, and I believe it is to be the one subject which, if studied practically, can be more benefited by honest industry in examination and intelligence in description than any other that refers either to the commercial or industrial pursuits of the Pacific coast. At the present time I am laboring under two great difficulties. First, many of the valuable detailed notes collected during the past four years, and appearing as memoranda in certain books that were inadvertently taken on the Colorado, were lost at the bottom of that river; and second, very many other later and duplicated notes are now *en route;* therefore memory has measurably to satisfy the claims that attach to this important subject.

The total number of mining districts within the area covered by the exploration was ninety-two, of which eighty-six were visited by some member or members of the expedition; of these fifty-seven are in Nevada, eighteen in California, seventeen in Arizona. In connection with those entered in 1869, my immediate attention has been called to more than one hundred districts, mostly of the silver-bearing ores. The location and size of all these appear on the map, and from it a great deal of valuable information regarding the practicability of reaching these districts, with a view to any mining operation, can be obtained.

Personal examinations were made in the mining districts by Lieutenants Lockwood and Lyle, Dr. Hoffman, and Civilian Assistant Gilbert, all of whom present memorandum reports. In some cases a topographical party alone visited the district. In order to facilitate the amount of information to be gained from the necessarily hasty examinations of many districts, lists of questions, forty-five in number, a copy of which is attached to show the character of the information that was obtained, were prepared, so as to be filled out while in the district. It will be attempted to duplicate as much as possible of the information to be gained hereafter, from the recorders or residents of the district, to replace that lost in the Colorado.

LIST OF QUESTIONS.

1. Date of discovery of this district.
2. Has the district been worked at intervals, or continuously, since that time ?
3. Name of recorder.
4. Name of postmaster.
5. Name of Wells, Fargo & Co.'s agent.
6. Distance from railroad communication, and nearest practicable route.
7. Description in detail of the geographical boundaries of the district.
8. Position of mining ledges in regard to the main range of mountains in vicinity, *i. e.,* whether in a cañon or along foot-hills; and, if the latter, on which slope. Give general trend of mountains in vicinity, as well as that of marked spurs, ridges, and foot-hills.
9. General direction of lodes, deposits, and stratifications.
10. In case there are any real or supposititious fissure-veins, or others of a permanent character, name the wall-rock, direction of the slopes, and planes of the hanging and foot-walls of the vein at different levels, and items of evidence of the existence of a permanent or regular vein. Amount and location of timber, wood, and water; this latter description in detail.
11. Geological age of the rocks in the vicinity of the mineral developments and their mineralogical characteristics. The nature and quantity of fossils, if any are found in the country rock.

12. Nature of ores in vicinity, i. e., whether they are worked by free or wet, roasting or smelting process, and average yield per ton.

13. Gross annual production of bullion from the mines, as well as that for each month of the year since the beginning, giving also the number of tons worked, as near as may be.

14. Average cost per ton for mining the ore.

15. Average cost per ton for milling the ore.

16. Average cost per ton for roasting the ore.

17. Average cost of mining labor, per diem.

18. Average cost of milling labor, per diem.

19. Cost of grain and hay; facilities for raising farm produce, stock, &c.

20. Number of mills and description of each, with the cost of, and amount of ore that each can work; this should give the weight of stamps and number of drops per minute, size of engine, number of boilers, number of pans and settlers, amalgamation process, and cold or hot straining of amalgam.

21. The principal mines now worked, with the description of each in detail.

22. Amount expended in the mineral development of any of the principal veins, and probable amount of bullion extracted from the same.

23. Number of inhabitants of the district.

24. Number of freight or stage lines.

25. Price of freight and passage from railroad.

26. Number of churches, school-houses, banking-houses, stores, &c.

27. Cost at the present time of a 10-stamp mill, with or without a Stedefeldt or other roasting furnace, also of an ordinary smelting furnace, in this district; this should itemize first cost of machinery, transportation to mill site, and construction account.

28. Average amount of ore that can be stoped by one man in one day.

29. Average amount of ore that can be extracted by one man in one day.

30. Whether tunnels should be run in vein matter or in the country rock.

31. Average cost per foot for running a tunnel on main veins.

32. Average cost per foot for sinking a shaft on main veins.

33. Average cost per foot for running a drift on a main vein.

34. As nearly as may be, the exact area in the district covered by the mineral croppings and developments, giving area in acres, shape of area, and trend of longer axis.

35. State as near as may be the real or supposititious water-level in the veins, and if the water-level has been reached, state whether there has been a change in the nature of the ore.

36. Is there any economical building-stone in the locality?

37. Are there any indications of coal in the neighborhood, or have any been reported?

38. How many head of stock in the vicinity, and are more coming in?

39. What kinds of game are found?

40. Nature of roads.

41. Names of Indian tribes, number of Indians, men, women, and children.

42. Do assays show the presence of gold in any of the silver-bearing ores in the district?

43. Procure copy of the mining laws of the district.

44. Chances for a decrease in the expense of any of the items incurred in mining industry.

45. Any proposition relative to a change in the mining laws, that shall give more certainty to the final acquirement of title and prevent chances of "jumping" and litigation.

In view of the present condition of the data in this matter, it seems proper to confine this report to circumstances concerning the locality of the various districts, the general character of the ores, the nature of the inclosing and country rock, the prospect of permanency in the veins, &c., and close the subject with a few suggestions and recommendations. Mr. Gilbert alone presents geological notes.

DISTRICTS IN NEVADA.

These will be mentioned sensibly in their order from north to south. Many of these districts are not new, having their place in reports already made and published, but, coming within the lines of the routes traversed, were always entered when opportunity occurred, with a view to record any change in the condition of the mining industry at the date of our visit.

The reports to which the above reference is made are those of the United States Commissioner of Mining Statistics, Vol. III of the Fortieth Parallel Geological Survey, and those of the State mineralogist of Nevada.

BULL RUN DISTRICT, NEVADA.

White Rock City, the principal location in this district, and the only one that is now active, is eighty-nine miles north from Carlin, on the Central Pacific Railroad. The connecting wagon-road, which is of fair quality, follows Maggie's Creek and Independence Valley. The Bull Run Range has a north and south trend, and forms the eastern limit of the broad valley of the Owyhee. At the point in question it consists chiefly of (1) a bluish-gray, bastard limestone, somewhat altered, checked by frequent veins of calcite running at all angles; (2) gray, impure quartzite, passing on the one hand into argillaceous schist, and on the other into impure sandstone, resting against (3) a gray, homogeneous, syenitic granite. The granite is seen along the western foot of the range, and in ascending to the divide one crosses the edges of the stratified beds, which rest against it, and dip at 30° to 60° to the east. A system of fissure veins substantially conforming to the dip and trend of the strata, traverses all the metamorphic beds, and even the granite, but is metalliferous only in the former. The metal mined is silver, and its principal associate is lead. So far as wrought, the veins have afforded chiefly oxidized ores, but some sulphides have been found, though the water-line has not yet been reached. There are no mills, and the ore is packed on mules to Cope district for reduction.

The principal mines in operation are the Central Pacific, Porter, and Town Treasure. The number of men employed is small, and the entire population does not exceed fifteen; the mines are comprised in an area two miles north and south by one mile east and west. There are no stage or freight lines. The best available building material is timber, with which White Rock Cañon is well supplied. Water for mill use is at hand, and at the cañon of Bull Run Creek, a few miles farther south, is an available mill-site, with water-power.[*]

A hurried personal visit was made to this locality, not so much, however, to examine the mines as to cross the divide of the waters of the Humboldt and Columbia Basins, and gain a look along the valley of the Owyhee, which observation alone paid for a long ride of nearly two hundred miles. The heavy snow on the mountains had not disappeared, and evidently the miners were waiting for the opening of the spring in order to commence vigorous work. Samples of ore, both chloride and sulphide, looked very promising, so far as this alone could show. The majority of the ores require roasting, and hence that heavy weight of expense per ton must act here, as it has so often in other regions, as an incubus to speedy developments. These mines had been opened but little at this date; however, it has since been understood that arrangements have been completed to bring in machinery, and, if the ore developments have kept pace, good test evidence will already have been furnished of what may be expected of this mining camp.

Poor placers have been found in the little basin to the eastward of the main range, but they have been abandoned as unprofitable. Similar placers, it is understood, have been slightly worked in the neighborhood of the mines at Cope district.

COPE DISTRICT, NEVADA.[†]

Discovered in 1869. Worked continuously since that interval. From Mountain City, the only mining camp in the district, to Elko, via the stage-road, the distance is ninety miles.

The ores are principally sulphurets. Fuel for roasting is abundant, at convenient places. Mining labor costs here $4.50 per day. There have been two large mills erected here, extracting some bullion.

The principal mines worked in June, 1871, are as follows: Mountain City, Pride of the West, Argenta, Excelsior, Independent, U. S. Grant, Eldorado, Crescent, Idaho, Nevada, Emmett, and Saint Nicholas. A study of names on the recorder's books of the many mining districts furnishes much of an index to the character of the miners and prospectors, who often place no little stress and pride upon the names selected with so much solicitude. Number of residents, about

---

[*] From notes furnished by Mr. G. K. Gilbert.
[†] From notes furnished by Mr. F. R. Simonton.

four hundred and fifty; one freight and one stage line to Elko. The country roads are good in this vicinity. The Shoshone Indians inhabit this locality, catching many salmon for themselves and the miners during the season. One of the forks of the head-waters of the Owyhee traverses this district. It is believed that many of the late developments do not favor the idea of permanency, although the present stage of the opening of the mines is not sufficiently advanced to warrant a definite conclusion.

Notes from J. W. Drew, late United States Army, give an altitude of 5,800 feet to the camp; also, average of temperatures, maximum and minimum, as occurring in July and December, former 84°, 21 F., latter 20°, 45 F. Snow liable to fall any time between November 1 and April 30.

LONE MOUNTAIN DISTRICT, NEVADA.

Situated in a rather isolated comb-shaped range, this district lies to the east of the head of Maggie Creek, and about forty-five miles from Carlin, on the Central Pacific Railroad; it is more approachable, however, from Elko, Nevada, via the stage-road to Cope district. The district was only visited by a topographical party. Very little work has been done on the mines, and but little prospecting even, in this locality. The majority of the ledges are noted as occurring on the eastern slope of the mountains. Some later prospects have been found on the western side, carrying argentiferous galena and carbonate ores, well charged with iron as both coloring and matrix matter. The specimens gathered from mines on the eastern side show galena and poor sulphuret ore, carrying considerable carbonate of copper. There is evidently a field for intelligent prospecting in this vicinity.

TUSCARORA DISTRICT, NEVADA.*

The Tuscarora placer mines are on the southward slope of hills of rhyolite, facing Independence Valley, and are fifty-six miles by road, north from Carlin Station. The dirt is derived from subjacent rock, and covers it to but a small depth in the gulches—5 to 10 feet. The gold has the same origin, and can be obtained in small quantity from the parent rock. Some spots showed so much as to induce the erection of a ten-stamp mill; but the amount extracted was not remunerative, and the mill is idle; there are no veins. The dirt is washed in sluices, with water brought two to six miles, the supply availing but three or four months. The gold is combined with silver, and brings $12 to $13 per ounce. The diggings occupy a belt one-half mile by two miles. Most of the miners are Chinamen, working in companies Population about one hundred and twenty-five. There is no timber convenient.

RAILROAD DISTRICT, NEVADA.

This district, situated south of Carlin, on the Central Pacific Railroad, and at a distance of twenty-one miles, was visited by a topographical party. Specimens collected. The notes are wanting. The district was established in June, 1870. The ores are very base, and should be more properly termed copper ores. They, however, carry average assays of silver, and in consequence of their proximity to the railroad, with which they are now connected by three good mountain roads, some, at least, of these properties will be profitably worked.

MINERAL HILL DISTRICT, NEVADA.

Discovered in June, 1869. It has been worked nearly continuously since that time.

A stage-line connects with Palisades on Central Pacific Railroad about thirty-one miles distant. The ledges are principally on the northwestern side of a conical-shaped hill, being an outlier to the west from the main mountains; direction of the mineral veins, northwest and southeast. The development that had taken place at the time of our visit did not show the best of indications for the presence of a permanent vein, but gave more the appearance of pockets in limestone, which exhaust, bringing up in their downward course upon the country rock. However, it is understood

---

* From notes furnished by Mr. G. K. Gilbert.

that at the White Pine district, after exhausting these basins, frequently others are found by sinking directly or following some mineral thread or discoloration. The ores belong to the base metal order, abounding in sulphurets of silver and lead and carbonate of copper. In order to extract an economic percentage, the roasting process has to be applied. The gross production up to June 1, 1871, or in two years, was $600,000; number of tons, 3,300; cost of mining the ore, per ton, $5; cost of milling the ore, including roasting, per ton, $30; mining and milling labor per diem, $4. There is one 15-stamp mill with a Stedefeldt furnace erected here at a total cost of $80,000; its capacity is 22 tons in twenty-four hours.

The principal mines worked are the Austin, Mary Ann, Rim Rock, Grant, Star of the West, Vallejo, and Pogonip; upon these mines, with the exception of the Austin, about $80,000 have been expended; returns $450,000; upon the Austin about $50,000 expended, returns so far $150,000. Number of inhabitants, four hundred and fifty nearly. One stage and a variety of freight-lines connect with the railroad. Cost of freight, 1 cent per pound. Stage fare, $8. The cost of a 10-stamp mill at this locality, with a Stedefeldt furnace, is estimated at $65,000, estimating $13,000 for the furnace; both this and the total amount being liberal estimates. The whole area covered by mineral croppings will hardly exceed one mile square. There is at present no indication of reaching a water-level. A species of natural fire-stone, valuable for the lining of the furnace, is found not far distant. Water is obtained in limited quantities in a cañon to the north and east, along which the little mining town has been built. Wood is not plenty in the immediate vicinity, though large tracts are in view upon the sides of the mountains to the north and east. The Shoshones inhabit this region, and work to a limited extent for the miners. The country roads in this vicinity are solid. When the local tariffs on the railroad and the price of labor diminish, many items that affect the cost of the extraction of the bullion at this comparatively accessible district will be cheapened. This district was visited by one of the members of the fortieth parallel geological survey. Many new developments have been made since that time.

DIAMOND DISTRICT, NEVADA.

.(Visited by a topographical party. Results from a few scattering notes.)

Situated on the western slope of the Diamond Range, north and west from Diamond Station, on the old overland stage-road. Diamond City is the name of the little camp. The Mammoth mine has been well opened by a shaft, now more than 75 feet. The elevation at the mouth of this shaft is 7,740 feet. The ore is principally argentiferous galena, giving assays as high as $270 per ton, and carrying 72 per cent. of lead. Veins run north and south, crossing an east and west stratified rock, about one and one-half miles in width. A smelting-furnace, soon to be in operation, was being built. The original locators, having wasted some money in improvements, abandoned afterward their claims. The principal locations are the Champion, Hidden Treasure, Patriot, Curtis, and Keller. The location of these mines in regard to the railroad and the high percentage of silver, ought to establish profitable enterprises in this district if the mines are systematically worked.

RACINE DISTRICT, NEVADA.

(From scattering notes by a topographical party.)

Situated about forty-five miles from Elko, on the western slope of the Humboldt Range, and east of Dutchman's Station on the White Pine stage-road. All the appurtenances for a mining camp are here abundant. Very little development made, and this only upon two mines—the Uncle Sam and De Witt. Elevation of mines, 7,440 feet; specimens show several varieties of base silver ores, and are all from the croppings. A little legitimate prospecting may find surface indications to warrant the investment of a certain amount of capital to determine the character of this area of mineral land.

This district lies on the stage-road from Palisades, on Central Pacific Railroad, to Hamilton, White Pine County, seventy-nine miles distant from the former station. The mines were first discovered in 1868, worked for a period, and then partially abandoned, after which, in the spring of 1870, developments were going on in full vigor. Seven furnaces were in operation, the most successful one at this time being that of the Eureka Consolidated Company. The mineral croppings of this region are strewn over a considerable space, with but little regularity of form. The lead-bearing ores predominate, while on the western slopes of the rolling mountains that face toward the southern end of Diamond Valley, milling ores are found, of both sulphide and chloride of silver, in limestone, however, and having no remarkable appearance of permanence. The ore that produces the best results from the smelting has a brownish, decomposed look, carrying much carbonaceous matter, and oftentimes not lead enough to facilitate the smelting process. The ore-beds defined seem to have a dip to the northeast of about 30^c, following wavy beds quite similar to what has been noticed in disturbed coal basins. The principal mines worked are those of the Eureka Consolidated Company, embracing one entire hill, joined at the southeast by properties of the Phœnix and Jackson Companies, the latter idle. Outside from these the Bull Whacker, Otto, Empire, and Lexington mines were visited, and samples of milling ores were taken from the Star of the West and General Lee. Various freight lines deliver stores for 1 cent per pound from railroad. The area covered by mines is most irregular in shape, but will approximate to eleven square miles. A volcanic granite quarry to the east of the town furnishes a fine quality of building material. Wood for charcoal is abundant among the hills, bordering a radius of eight to ten miles. No records on hand at present give the annual production of bullion. The amount from the Ely Consolidated, running five furnaces, has often reached, if not exceeded, $175,000 per month. The present price for freight on bullion is $10 per ton, to the railroad. Several freight lines compete. The town of Eureka is a very lively and smoky one; several hotels, one church, one bank, and one school-house are found here. The Richmond furnace is the only one that has a refinery attached.

(Notes from a topographical party.)

Situated south and east from Eureka, about twelve miles distant. Rich cropping found and several mines worked with great success. From the Geddis mines, Nos. 3 and 4, ore taken from a shaft over 70 feet in depth has milled an average of $225—rich bodies bringing out results very much superior to this. The Calico mine has a shaft of 75 feet, showing average milling ore of $100. Shafts have also been sunk to good depths on the Bertram, and Geddis Nos. 1 and 2, Secret Valley, Stockton, and some others. The district, though small and comparatively new, has an air of good promise.

The cost of the various items pertaining to mining industry varies but little if any from that at Eureka, near at hand.

(Notes from a topographical party.)

This little mining camp is situated at the entrance to a wide cañon on the eastern slope of the Diamond Range, among the foot-hills of which the mines are located, lying in a southeasterly direction, and not far from Eureka.   Specimens obtained were from the Maryland mine; others forwarded from this district have not been received for examination, but are taken from the Mountain Chief, Michigan, Uncle Sam, Duquette, Cole & Johnson, and Our Own, No. 2, mines.   The ores are chlorides and sulphurets of silver, with galena interspersed; a part can be smelted; it is maintained that others can be worked by the wet or free process; course of veins northeast and southwest.

Water is scarce, and at a distance from the mines.   Wood for fuel purposes plenty.   The several expenses of mining industry vary but slightly from those obtained in Eureka.

MOREY DISTRICT, NEVADA.

The mines of this district are north of Hot Creek, the camp itself lying to the south of Eureka, a distance of seventy-five miles, and south and west from Hamilton, at a distance of sixty-one miles. The ledges are arranged in a parallel system of thin fissures, found in the foot-hills, whose trend is south 55° west magnetic, and which form a portion of the eastern slope of the Hot Creek Range. The mines are found on either side of these hills, nearly uniform in direction, converging slightly to the main peak of the contiguous ridge; these foot-hills break off to the northeast from the main range.   General trend of the mountains north and south.   The country rock is somewhat disturbed, and much *débris* from the peaks to the southwest covers the surface.   Bearing of lodes south 55° west; country rock is an ancient volcanic rock, probably propylite, with later introduced volcanic dikes.   The veins have an average dip of 60°   No vein has been found to exhaust either in horizontal or vertical working.   Some veins are perpendicular.   Plenty of nut-pine and cedar for fuel and timbering in adjoining hills; fine building-stone in cañon one and a half miles to the south; three springs of fine water in the district.   The ores are all high grades, associated with manganese, and require roasting.   The Stedefeldt process has been found to give a high percentage at Austin.   Average cost of mining per ton, $25; price of mining and milling labor, $4.   As yet there is no mill, although the developments justly merit one.

Principal mines worked: Magnolia, Bay State, Cedar, and American Eagle.   Total amount of bullion for nine months ending June 30, 1871, $27,500, giving an average of $315 per ton. Freight to Austin, 3½ cents; to Eureka this might be reduced to 2 cents.   The cost of a 10-stamp mill and Stedefeldt furnace is estimated at $45,000; this is a low estimate.   The ore from these mines has been transported to Austin at a great expense and there worked; meanwhile the district has been self-supporting to the Morey Company, they being the only ones who have done much work.   In their case, however, it has been conducted on a very small scale.   The total number of feet owned by them is 20,400; this embraces the greater share of the district, which is quite small.   The matrix material of the veins is soft.   The introduction of Chinese labor succeeded satisfactorily at this point while it was tried by Mr. D. S. Ogden, the superintendent, and was only discontinued at the time it was concluded to lessen operations.

This labor ought to be introduced to a certain limited extent among the mines of the interior, where cheap labor is so much needed.   By arranging them in small gangs, placing over each an intelligent and vigilant foreman, the work can be equally as well done.   They also succeed well as assorters of ore.   The veins are from 3½ to 5 feet thick, showing a pay-streak from 6 to 22 inches, and giving assays from $75 to $525.   Work was being pushed ahead on the Cedar and Magnolia at the date of our visit, and from the latter the most flattering results obtained at the end of the tunnel, 155 feet.   Ore from a pay-streak from 18 inches to 2½ feet was continuously averaging from $150 to $200 per ton, and often reaching as high as $600.

The Bay State, Mount Airy, American Eagle, and Black Hawk are all good mines.   The average milling results, after little assorting, average from $395 to $552 per ton.   Quite thorough examinations were made here, and the impressions produced were exceedingly favorable; indeed, there are few localities yet encountered where there is a more favorable opportunity for the judicious expenditure of capital.

WHITE PINE DISTRICT, NEVADA.

No examinations made here since 1869, subsequent to which visit there was a great lull in mining matters; latterly, however, the prospects have greatly revived; mines have been found to descend where alone pockets were expected; capital has been introduced on a large and liberal scale. I am informed that the charter has been granted and the incorporation perfected for a narrow-gauge railroad from Elko to Hamilton, and that work is soon to be commenced. A wire tramway for transporting the ore from the mine to the mill at a trifling expense is in operation, and at last accounts was working successfully. This is the first instance in which this method of transporting the ores has been tried; various experiments are going on with a view to perfect this sort of a tramway, and the results cannot fail to be a step in the right direction.

SPRING VALLEY DISTRICT, NEVADA.

This district is situated immediately north of the stage-road from Austin to Eureka and about twelve miles from the latter place. The ores are chlorides and sulphides of silver in metamorphic limestone, showing croppings of a limited size. But little labor has been applied, and beyond generalizations of the widest nature, but little can be said. Most of the miners were absent and the time for observation short. The mines lay in the southeastern foot-hills, covered with nut pine. Water is scarce. The country roads are good.

ANTELOPE DISTRICT, NEVADA.

Situated about fourteen miles in a southwest direction from Mineral Hill. Base metal ore in a highly metamorphic limestone formation. No developments showing expectations even of a permanent vein. The croppings are distributed over a considerable area, among low, rolling hills, on the western slope of a range that passes nearly due south from Mineral Hill. Water scarce; wood plenty. A few miners at work.

HOT CREEK AND EMPIRE DISTRICTS.

Situated in the Hot Creek Range, and successively to the south and adjoining Morey. These localities were visited by topographical parties, but no notes are available except the average milling assays of the ores from the Hot Creek district at the Old Dominion mill, when this was in operation. These were very favorable, in no month falling below $200 per ton, and reaching as high as $325 per ton. The mines are on the eastern slope of the range, and crop from a volcanic formation. A transcript from the mill returns of the Old Dominion mill shows the average working value per ton to range from $80 to $472.

RATTLESNAKE CAÑON DISTRICT, NEVADA.

South of Empire, adjoining it, and now believed to be a part of it; is being worked by a New York company, whose principal endeavors have attached to the Philadelphia mine; showing roasting ores, stedefeldtite predominating. The ore deposits are in volcanic rock. The water-level had been reached, and arrangements were soon to be made for pumping, when it was intended to push the work on with vigor. The walls, at a depth of 55 feet, were clean and well defined. Water sufficient for mining purposes. Wood scarce. No mill in the cañon. A 2-stamp mill in sight in the valley below.

TYBOE DISTRICT, NEVADA.

The little mining camp of this name is situated in a cañon that runs toward the Hot Creek Valley, and from the mountains between the Rattlesnake Cañon and the old Milk Spring district. This district shows two very dissimilar series of ores. The first, prominent along a very long line of east and west croppings, is of a yellowish-brown ore, heavily charged with lead, assaying about $60 per ton in silver, and, like the Eureka ores, can doubtless be easily smelted. The ores from the west, and in the direction of the Empire Cañon, show sulphide and chloride of silver in limestone, and also among volcanic rocks. The first series belong to a line of fissure; the others have no particular direction, and doubtless are pockets for the greater part. The veins of the carbonaceous ores are wide. Several miners were vigorously at work; wood and water sufficient for mining purposes. The most direct access to this locality is via Eureka, and thence down Hot Creek Valley. The distance from Hot Creek Station is fourteen miles. But few developments had been made. The principal work has been done on the 2 G, Casket, and Western Extension mines. The district is, however, in my mind, one of great promise, if developments prove that it can be worked on a large and comprehensive scale. The direction of the veins trends toward the summit of the range. The nearest milling center at present is Belmont. Plenty of wood for fuel purposes. Roads are not yet well opened.

BATTLE MOUNTAIN DISTRICT, NEVADA.*

The district includes four principal locations, known as Battle Mountain, Trenton, Galena, and Copper Cañon, all on the eastern slope of the Battle Mountain Range. The first mentioned, which is the oldest, I did not visit. Galena, five miles farther south, is now the principal center of activity; it is situated fourteen miles south from Battle Mountain Station, with which it is connected by a good road. The country rocks are metamorphic sedimentary, (quartzite, mica-slate, clay-slate, limestone, &c.,) dipping to the west at all angles, from 20° to 75°. The veins are well defined, and for the most part are more nearly vertical than the adjacent beds, but trend with them north and south.

The chief ore is argentiferous galena, and some mines have passed below the water-level; others are still dry and yield a large proportion of oxidized ores. Price of labor, $3.50 *per diem*. No mill was in operation at the time of my visit, but that of the Nevada Butte Silver Mining Company approached completion. The best ore ($150 to $300 per ton) is shipped to San Francisco.

The principal mines worked are the Avalanche, Buena Vista, Butte, Trinity, and White, and they are comprised in an area about one and one-half miles square. Population, 200.

The mines of Copper Cañon (the Virgin and Lake Superior) lie three miles farther south, and are worked entirely for copper. The surface ores are carbonate of copper and red oxide, and the deep-seated copper glance. The water-level has not been reached. The ore is sold in Liverpool.

Galena and Copper Cañon have a scant supply of water, and have no timber in the immediate vicinity, though it is found on the range.

YANKEE BLADE DISTRICT, NEVADA.*

Situated immediately north of the Reese River district. It is reported at Austin that work has been entirely suspended in this district.

REESE RIVER DISTRICT, NEVADA.*

There are no new developments at Austin, but, by economic and skillful management, the place is recovering from the stagnation that followed the White Pine excitement. The mill of the Manhattan Company, which now does a large custom business in addition to the reduction of the ores mined by the company, is to be enlarged, and another mill is building to reduce, by competition, the prices of milling, and foster still further the development of mines held by parties with small capital. Great advantage is derived in the large mines from the use of a contract system, which pays the miners in whole or part by a percentage of the ore extracted.

---

* From notes furnished by Mr. G. K. Gilbert.

KINGSTON DISTRICT, NEVADA.*

Situated on the eastern flank of the Toyabe Range, twenty miles south of Austin. The silver mines of the district are entirely deserted, and the machinery of its mill is being removed.

NORTH TWIN RIVER DISTRICT, NEVADA.*

Situated on the eastern flank of the Toyabe Range, facing Smoky Valley, and thirty-five miles south of Austin. The great speculations that have been based on this district are without fulfillment. In Summit Cañon, two men are said to be at work, and at the entrance of Park Cañon, where stands an unfinished silver-reducing mill, the proprietor still faithfully maintains his residence.

TWIN RIVER DISTRICT, NEVADA.*

Situated immediately south of North Twin River district, and including Twin River, Last Chance, Ophir, and Wisconsin Cañons. In Ophir Cañon the extensive works of the Twin River Silver Mining Company stand idle, the celebrated Murphy mine is full of water, and the town, once containing several hundred, has now but five or six inhabitants, two of whom are engaged in mining. The other cañons are quite deserted.

JEFFERSON DISTRICT, NEVADA.*

This district of silver mines is situated on the west side of the Toquima Mountains, being separated by that range from the Silver Bend District, (Belmont,) and by the Smoky Valley from the Twin River district, (Ophir Cañon.) It is entirely deserted.

MANHATTAN DISTRICT, NEVADA.*

This district, now abandoned, was located on the west side of the Toquima Mountains, immediately south of the Jefferson district.

MOUNTAIN CHIEF DISTRICT, NEVADA.

This district, visited by a topographical party, lies on the eastern slope of the Toquima Range, and nearly due north from our camp at Meadow Creek Cañon. Principal mines: Mountain Chief, Mount Ruby, and Blue Point; no notes available.

SILVER BEND DISTRICT, NEVADA.

Belmont stands on a system of plicated black shales of silurian age, with some associated limestone and quartzite, all dipping east and northeast at high angles, and resting against a mass of granite that lies west and south of them. The argentiferous veins are near the granite, and dip and trend with the strata.*

Quite a minute survey and examination were made in this locality by members of the fortieth parallel geological survey, and there is little left to be done beyond chronicling changes in the material developments of the mines that have since taken place. Nothing has been done with the mining or mill property of the combination company. Mr. Canfield had in constant operation a 10-stamp mill, with furnace and crushers, working upon ores from the Arizona and Transylvania mines, and paying a good profit.

The owners of the El Dorado south were busily engaged in a legitimate development of their mine down to the water-level, which shows at this point a most beautiful fissure-vein.

The old Belmont mill, situated in the town of Belmont, was receiving a thorough overhauling, preparatory to receiving new furnaces and machinery. The ore supply was expected to come from explorations that had commenced on the Transylvania north, and upon the old Belmont lead.

The Monitor, in the bight of the hill near the summit, and lying nearly in a line between the Arizona and El Dorado south shafts, was taking out fine, high-grade ore. Other parties, here and there, were prospecting their leads in a small way.

---

* From notes furnished by Mr. G. K. Gilbert.

To the north and west of the town, and in the continuation of the mineral-bearing trend, some mines were visited. At one of them a little work is progressing. They doubtless belong to the same system of mineral deposition.

Mining and milling labor commands $3.50 per day. There are sixty stamps set up in this district, only ten of which were working.

Two freight-lines connect with Austin. Number of inhabitants, 400.

There is said to have been taken out, in bullion, from the High Bridge, $170,000; El Dorado, $200,000, and Transylvania, $250,000. During the last year the bullion from the Arizona has increased the above amount, so that probably the district in total has produced not far from $750,000. The veins here are undoubtedly permanent. The range of the properties is limited. Developments become exceedingly expensive after reaching the water-level.

By the judicious combination of interests and application of capital, this could be made one of the most flourishing districts in the interior of Nevada. The original name of this district was Silver Bend, then it was temporarily called Philadelphia; at present the record-books show "Silver Bend" to be the appropriate name.

REVEILLE DISTRICT, NEVADA.*

Reveille district, organized in 1856, is on the Reveille Range, two hundred and twenty miles south, by road, from Elko, on the Central Pacific railroad. The mountains are here composed of heavy beds of lime and quartzite, uplifted and shattered by massive eruptions of rhyolitic lava. Silver ore has been found at numerous points in the surface of the limestone, with a calcareo-siliceous gangue, but no traceable vein has been demonstrated, except along the uneven margin of the rhyolite, where it is adjacent to the limestone. The base metals are iron, copper, lead, and antimony. No deep mining has been done, but a notable amount of superficial work. A mill for the district was built twelve miles west, at the foot of the Hot Creek Range, but it is not now used, and the district is quiescent. The supplies of water and timber are scant.

FREIBERG DISTRICT, NEVADA.

This was formerly known as the Worthington district, and it is situated northwest from Silver Cañon, about seventeen miles distant. The ores are represented as rich smelting ores. The notes taken by C. A. Ogden are not now available. It is understood that the main mountains are of limestone, highly fossiliferous, covered on their eastern flanks by eruptive beds of rhyolite.

The deposits occur on the eastern base, cutting across the ravines that are parallel with the northeast spurs. Water in two places for mills; timber sufficient for fuel and building purposes. The area covered by croppings is about 2½ square miles.

ELY DISTRICT, NEVADA.

The range, or group of hills occupied by the district stands as an island on the eastern foot-slopes of the Ely Mountain Range, and is quite as peculiar in structure as in position, since its axis of elevation and the accompanying fractures trend north 60° west, and the system of argentiferous veins east and west, nearly at right angles to the general trend of the Cordilleras. The rocks are slightly altered limestone and argillaceous shale, with vitreous sandstone or quartzite. At Pioche the latter stretches as a longitudinal belt, a half mile in width, with an easy dip to the northeast, and is separated by faults from bodies of limestone and shale on either side, through which it seems to have been uplifted. The metalliferous veins are confined to this belt. In the shale a few fossils were found, one of which I thought to be a Carboniferous form, (*Phillipsia*,) but, as the specimens were afterward destroyed, it has been impossible to confirm this identification.*

This district, first discovered in 1864, was relocated, and developments commenced in 1868. A visit was made here in the fall of 1868, since which time astonishing developments have been made, and Pioche ranks second to no mineral section in Nevada, except Washoe. Fifty-five stamps were busily employed, the ore being worked by what is known as the wet process, giving a fair percentage;

---

* From notes furnished by Mr. G. K. Gilbert.

the tailings are collected, however, and will be reworked at some later period. Only the higher-grade ores are carried to the mill at the present stage of the mining industry. Water being very scarce in the mines, the mills have had to be erected, one in Dry Valley, about eight miles to the eastward, others at Bullionville, eleven miles to the south. The present cost of transportation of ores from the mine to the mill is somewhat of a burden. The wall-rock is quartzite, badly broken and disturbed in many places; the ores found are chloride and sulphuret of silver; specimens of horn and ruby silver, stedefeldtite, argentiferous galena, small amounts of manganate of silver, oxide and carbonate of lead, and pyrites of iron. The lower levels have a tendency toward sulphuret ores, and it is not unlikely that, at no distant date, in order to secure a sufficiently high percentage, roasting will have to be introduced.

The main veins occupy but a small lateral extension, separating, a short distance from the western end, into two branches or prongs, or, looking from the other extremity, these prongs uniting ought to lead to a wide and more substantial vein to the westward.

Astonishing results have been obtained from the (Lightener) shaft, sunk on the Raymond and Ely property in this direction, $750,000 having been taken out, at a profit to the stockholders of more than $450,000, in four months. The principal companies are the Meadow Valley, Raymond and Ely, and Pioche. Other parties have lately made developments, some of which are reported as of good promise.

This district was the scene of considerable terror and bloodshed for quite a season, caused by the disputes and litigations arising from frequent "jumping" of claims. Much of the blackmailing spirit has held sway, and may be cited as an instance of the loose state in which mining laws, records, titles, &c., are often placed, incident upon the irregular method of the prospecting, locating, and placing in market of mines in interior and remote sections.

The little town of Pioche, in July, 1871, was as thriving, cleanly, and well-regulated a mining town as it has been in my experience to meet. A fire, in August, destroyed nearly everything, and left the surface of the country more desolate than before the mines were worked; since that time the enterprise that is evinced in all mining camps where bullion is produced has put together a new town of as respectable proportions as the former.

Several boxes of valuable fossils, and collections in natural history, *en route*, were destroyed in this fire.

HIGHLAND DISTRICT, NEVADA.

This lies to the west of Pioche, Nevada, and is understood to be in a limestone formation. Most promising specimens of ore from this locality were seen. It is believed that there are some good properties here. It is understood that a 30-stamp mill is about to be erected. The notes taken by a topographical party are not at hand.

BLIND MOUNTAIN DISTRICT, NEVADA.

North and west from the Highland, carrying base-metal ores; little prospected, and very little work being done. Mining laws very good; plenty of wood, but water scanty. Notes from a topographical party not at hand.

CEDAR DISTRICT, NEVADA.

This district was discovered in 1871, and lies on the western side of Bennett Spring Mountains, and nearly due east from Pahranagat Lake. Most of the assays, so far as could be found out, showed only a low-grade silver ore. The locality was not visited from want of time.

PAHRANAGAT LAKE DISTRICT, NEVADA.

Great Quartz Mountain is a mass of uplifted and somewhat altered strata, with a general dip to the west. The quartzite, 500 to 600 feet thick, that caps the ridge, are of slight inclination, exposing their edges on both sides of the mountain, and they contain an interstratified bed of black limestone. Below them is an almost uninterrupted exposure of limestone, to the eastern base of the mountain, and in these are the mines. They are so much disturbed and faulted that the thickness of the mass cannot be definitely ascertained, but it can hardly be less than 2,000 feet. The limestones are profusely fossiliferous, and belong to the Hudson River and Trenton groups of the Silurian system.*

The district of Pahranagat Lake, once the scene of great activity and excitement, is now comparatively deserted, except by a few persons known as "chloriders," who here and there coyote little pockets of rich ore, and take it to the Crescent mill, where it can be worked by the wet process.

The mill of the Hyko Silver Mining Company, who at one time spent their money here in so princely a manner, although well appurtenanced in every particular, now stands idle; though why, it is difficult to say. From a careful examination of this district, the presence of a great deal of surface mineral has been definitely determined; it has also been found out that former labors have been directed independent of sense or judgment.

The metamorphic limestone is greatly disturbed, and the tracing of the veins through it is very difficult. In the northern part of the district, spread over a considerable area, and cropping from the quartzite, other portions of this apparently large mineral deposit are found. It seems patent that success alone is to come from this portion of the extensive property, and it is my belief that no permanent and remunerative vein will be opened in the district until the croppings in the quartzite are tried. Verifying this opinion, formed while in the district, a shaft has been sunk in this locality, and good results obtained, although it had not reached over seventy feet at the date of the information.

It is rumored that the New York Company are soon to resume operations, and Pahranagat may yet add its history to that of the mining centers of the West. A bed of volcanic tufa at Logan Spring can furnish very superior building-stone.

TIM-PAH-UTE DISTRICT, NEVADA.

This district lies nearly due west from Silver Cañon, occupying the southwestern end of a detached range, similar to the Worthington Range. The eastern limit of the mineral-bearing zone is highly metamorphosed slate, with north and south stratification, parallel to which, and protruding through limestone, the country rock is a parallel quartzite dike, extending laterally for miles. Most of the leads are found between the quartzite and the slate, although stringers and seams of the ore are in the quartzite. It was supposed at one time that there was an immense vein of ore through the district, and that the Inca lode was this mother vein. Very few developments had been made to determine this, however, and nothing certain has been shown beyond a few narrow and rich leads. Several miners are laboring with a laudable vivacity, and it is hoped that their endeavors will be happily rewarded. Most of the miners are poor, and capital is sadly needed among the many forbidding localities in which mines are found. The ores average high grade, and considerable bullion has already been produced at the Crescent Mill and at Hyko.

GROOM DISTRICT, NEVADA.

The rocks are sedimentary, and comprise a series of thin-bedded, vitreous, red sandstone, overlaid by a mass of soft argillaceous and chloritic shales, succeeded in turn by massive gray and black limestones. These all trend north and south with the general course of the range, and dip to the east at an average angle of 30°. The several strata are to be seen, in the order named, by crossing the range from west to east, the sandstones and limestones, in virtue of their superior hardness, standing in bold ridges on either side of the eroded shale. By a succession of vertical faults carrying down the more easterly beds, the minor features are several times repeated, and the superficial width of the several members increased.

---

* From notes furnished by Mr. G. K. Gilbert.

Parallel with this system of faults, and within the shales, are the metalliferous deposits. Interstratified with the same shales are a few feet of limestone containing fossils of the Potsdam epoch. This is, I believe, the first recorded occurrence in the great basin of argentiferous veins in primordial rocks.*

This is an argentiferous galena district, and is situated south and west from Tim-pah-ute Peak. The mines occur in a system of parallel veins or deposits, from 75 to 200 feet wide, and show large amounts of ore. The galena is bright and lustrous, and carries in its composition little or no fluxing agent.

The surrounding hills are covered with nut-pine and cedar. The ores are of low grade, but the resulting lead should be of economic value. These ores will have to pass through a scorifying process before they can be introduced into a blast-furnace, and need, in connection, some fluxing agent. Whether nature has furnished that in the near vicinity has not yet been determined. Should this be found, and thorough proof adduced that the problem of smelting these ores can be solved on the ground, there seems to be no reason why, if this district were operated on a large scale, it should not be equally as profitable as the mines of Cerro Gordo. Cost of mining, $2 per ton. Mining labor, $4 per day. About $7,000 have been expended on the mines, developing continuance to 50 feet in depth.

SOUTHEASTERN DISTRICT, NEVADA.†

Work, on a small scale, has been carried on at intervals in this district since its discovery, in the spring of 1870. The nearest water is to the northwest about twelve miles. The situation of the mines is to the southeast from Tim-pah-ute Peak, in a cañon on the western slope of the northern end of the Vegas Range. Veins have appearance of permanency; ores of low grade. Ores are base, the principally associated metal being copper. Plenty of wood for mining purposes.

WAUCOVA DISTRICT, CALIFORNIA.

This district is nearly due east from Camp Independence about twenty-two miles, and on the eastern slope of the Inyo Range.

The mines were not examined by any members of the party; however, from the specimens and description, I am led to believe that they resemble, to a certain extent, those at Cerro Gordo that have been made so profitable. They are of argentiferous galena principally, some indifferent silver rock being exposed in places. But little work has been done so far. Wood and water are plenty. These mines may probably be made remunerative if worked on an extensive scale.

SAN ANTONIO DISTRICT, NEVADA.‡

We left San Antonio on the following morning, (July 5,) and traveled in a southeasterly direction for about nine miles. The soil at first was sandy, with "sage bushes" growing in abundance. When we had gone about six miles the soil became more barren and the vegetation scant. Here we came across volcanic ashes, with large quantities of fragments of agate, silicified wood, and lava. In the spring of 1864 J. P. Cortez & Co. opened the first mine, soon after which the district was formed. This mine was the La Libertad, which was soon followed by the Potomac, the Merrimac, and the Lea; and the whole number of claims in the district numbered about two hundred and fifty. San Lorenzo, or the old Potomac Camp, is a small, deserted village among a series of hills in a small valley, altitude 6,600 feet, (aneroid barometer 57.) We went southward in this small valley, in a gradual ascent, for about three-fourths of a mile, then descended again for the same distance to the Potomac. The general stratification of all the rocks runs northwest and southeast.

The tunnel is in the side of the hill, penetrating the stratifications at nearly a right angle east 40° north, to a depth of 300 feet through quartz.

The ores are cupreous sulphurets, also malachite and films of azurite. About fifty tons of ore have been taken out, averaging, without assorting, $100 per ton. This tunnel was intended to touch or penetrate the Jupiter lode; altitude at mouth of tunnel, 6,622 feet. Southeast of this, about 200 yards, is the Merrimac, not worth mentioning.

---

* From notes furnished by Mr. G. K. Gilbert.
† From notes furnished by Mr. F. R. Simonton.
‡ From notes furnished by Dr. W. J. Hoffman.

We now proceeded to the La Libertad, which is the most southern mine of the district. The entrance to the mine is an incline at an angle of 43°, altitude 5,710 feet, to a depth of 500 feet. At 400 feet we came to moist earth, and at a depth of 460 or 475 feet to water, which fills the bottom of the mine. Here we came to a drift running northwest to a distance of 50 feet. The quantity of ore taken out is about 300 tons. Cost of mining, $25 per ton ; cost of shipping, $25 per ton ; cost of working, $25 per ton. The amount derived since opening, about $100,000, which is not quite equal to the sum expended.

MONTEZUMA DISTRICT, NEVADA.*

(Camp in Big Smoky Valley, July 7, 1871.)

We left camp soon after sunrise for Montezuma, which was but eight miles southwest, on the northern slope of Mount Nagle, in a small ravine. In the valley we were just leaving was a salt-marsh, which is separated from the Silver Peak salt-marsh by a low divide of volcanic rocks, a continuation of Lone Mountain, with these mountains surrounding Montezuma. This district was discovered May 18, 1867, and was organized on May 24, 1867. The district has been worked constantly since that time. The recorder is Matthew Plunket. The nearest post-office is Silver Peak. The general course of the mining and other ledges is east 35° north and west 35° south. Incline of strata, 48°. The High Bridge mine follows down between two strata of metamorphic limestone, in which was embolite, (chloro-bromide of silver,) to a depth of 85 feet. Value, from $68 to $200 per ton. Altitude of opening, 6,950 feet. South of the town of Montezuma (which consists of six houses, two taverns, and a store, besides one dwelling-house, and a mill) lie the mines on the hill-side. The Savage mine, the most important in the place, has a tunnel of 80 feet depth to a silver-bearing vein, whose dip is at an angle of 40°.

The altitude of mouth of tunnel is 7,010 feet, (aneroid barometer 57.) The ores are embolite, sulphurets, malachite, azurite, (scarce,) selenite, chafazite, and a few of the rare zeolites. The principal mines are the Crocket, Mountain Queen, Brewster, and Osceola. The other mines of importance are the Hubbard, Norfolk, Southern, Light, Burchard, &c. There are about fifty claims in the district, nine of which have been worked at different times. The timber is abundant all over the mountains, but water is taken from wells. There is a 10-stamp mill erected at the camp, (dry stamp,) with a reverberatory furnace. This is also deserted at present. There are a few Indians living in the mountains. They appear to be at peace with all, and are often hired to carry water, wood, and do other work around the mines. Most miners get from $75 to $100 per month, with board. There has been expended in the development of the Crocket, $2,500 ; Mountain Queen, $8,000 ; Brewster, $3,000 ; and Osceola, $2,500. The ores are worked at Benton and Columbus.

BLIND SPRING DISTRICT, CALIFORNIA.*

This district was organized in the autumn of 1864. Distance from Reno one hundred and eighty-five miles, and Wadsworth one hundred and sixty-five miles. The mountain and ledges run north and south. There is one fissure-vein called the Comanche. This has not been sufficiently developed to give entire proof as such. No wood found here, and water occurs only in the valleys, from four to six miles away. The ores are antimoniates of lead and silver, and are extremely rich in silver. The yield for 1871 was $60,000. Cost of mining is $10 per ton ; cost of milling and chloridizing, $15 per ton ; labor per diem, $4 ; labor per month, $60, with board.

In the district near Benton is one 4-stamp mill, built at a cost of $4,000. It is run by water-power. This mill can work one and a half tons per day, (of ore.) The principal mines are the Comanche, Rockingham, Diana, and Silver Sprout, also the Wilson Claim, and Cornucopia. Costs of developing the claims are as follows : Comanche, $15,000 ; Rockingham, $12,000 ; Diana, $40,000 ; Wilson Claim, $7,000 ; Cornucopia, $60,000—not worked now ; Silver Sprout $2,000 ; Kearsarge, $15,000.

Late advices show a great change in the character of the ores in the Rockingham mine. At the time of visiting this place the water-level had not yet been reached, and the antimoniates of silver abounded exclusively. But upon reaching the water-level, at a depth of about 350 feet, the antimoniates were gradually replaced by the sulphurets, pyrites frequently occurring.

Partzwick has about ten buildings, of which one is a livery-stable, one store, and one liquor store and hotel ; number of inhabitants about forty. They are erecting at the northern end of the village a 10-stamp mill, with a Stedefeldt furnace, with capacity of working 15 tons of ore per day.

Benton is situated about a half mile south of Partzwick, and has—houses, 12 ; inhabitants, 55 ; blacksmith's shop, 1 ; hotel, 1 ; stores, 2 ; saloons, 2 ; livery-stable, 1 ; school-house, 1 ; Wells, Fargo & Co.'s office ; post-office. Also 1 arrastra mill, (water-power).

---

* From notes furnished by Dr. W. J. Hoffman.

ALIDA DISTRICT, NEVADA.*

Alida Valley is from one to two miles broad, by about six miles in length. At the extreme eastern part is located the spring, from which issues a fine stream of water. At the summit we just crossed we found a large vein of malachite and black oxide of copper croppings. The ravines on both sides of the mountain are covered with cedars and pines in abundance, and on the northern side of the mountain we saw two springs of good water. Alida Valley is covered with good grass, and the watercourse is fringed with a dense undergrowth of willows. Here a man named Scott was working a claim which he had discovered. The ore was stromeyerite, with malachite, cuprite, and a little hematite.

GOLD MOUNTAIN DISTRICT, NEVADA.*

We followed a trail up a wash, which took us just to the east of Mount Magruder, then down a gentle slope, and across a barren desert. Finally, after crossing two ranges of mountains, we came to another sand desert. Up the opposite side of this we came to Camp Gold Mountain, which is situated on the northern slope of Gold Mountain. The well at Gold Mountain Camp furnishes just sufficient water for the three men and four animals that are kept there. The district was formed in 1865. The nearest place for mail and freight-shipping is at Silver Peak. The nearest railroad station is Battle Mountain. Wood is abundant, and water can only be obtained on the northern slope of the mountain by sinking wells. On the southern slope, in a ravine, is East Spring, of alkaline water. The chief ore is gold, and for the purpose of reducing this an arrastra has been erected, and gold is obtained by means of amalgamation. Cost of mining the ore is about $10 per ton. Barley is worth 10 cents per pound, and hay is worth $50 per ton. There is sufficient grass on the mountain-slopes to furnish all pasture necessary for the animals. The amount realized for one month's work is $400, and two hundred pounds of rock is generally worked per day. The chief mines are the Evening Star, State Line, Nova Zembla, Kohinoor, Golden Eagle, Bamboo, Boomerang, Little Bell, Huburmac, and Borneo. The total number of locations is about forty. The amount expended since 1865 is about $7,000. There are but two men working at present, but at one time there were twenty employed. A 10-stamp mill would cost in this place $10,000 or $15,000. Many of the mines are situated on the slopes of the smaller mountains, which generally run east and west. Much gold is taken out of the summit of one mountain of syenite. The gold occurs in quartz, jasper, and malachite; specimens of the latter are unique. Argentiferous selenite, of excellent quality, occurs in abundance four miles south of camp. The State Line ledge, lying five miles to the northwest, is 3,000 feet in length, and 20 feet thick, yielding $20 per ton. The ledge runs northwest and southeast.

PALMETTO DISTRICT, NEVADA.*

This district was formed on April 9, 1866. Nearest place of communication is Silver Peak. The nearest railroad staion is Wadsworth. The ledges run north-northwest and south-southeast, and dip at an angle of 45° northeast. Abundance of timber, and several springs of water, and small streams two miles east. The number of tons of ore taken from the mines is about 500. Cost of mining ore is $12 per ton; cost of milling and roasting, $35 per ton; cost of chloridizing, $15 per ton; labor per day, mining, $4; labor per day, milling, $4; cost of barley, per pound, 5 cents; cost of hay, per ton, $50. There is one 10-stamp mill here, which cost $90,000.

The principal mines.—On the western slope of the range are the New York, Champion, Kentucky, and Virginia, supposed to be the same vein.

Those on the east are the Tennessee, Palmetto, Carolina, and Louisiana. The amount expended in these mines is $75,000, and bullion obtained about $200,000. A 10-stamp mill at present would cost about $36,000. The valley contains large quantities of grass, and is generally on limestone and sandy soil. Farther to the west are large quantities of porphyritic granite, containing fine crystallizations of orthoclase.

GREEN MOUNTAIN DISTRICT, NEVADA.

This district lies to the south of Palmetto, and is at present deserted. It was organized in 1869. The cost of working is the same as in Palmetto. The gold which was worked chiefly amounted to about $2,000. The only silver ledge in the district, the Veta Madre, runs northwest and southeast, and dips east. This lies between limestone and granite strata. The once famous Tule Cañon belongs to Green Mountain district. A part of the old Cottonwood district belongs to the Palmetto. In the latter district are about one hundred and twenty-five claims. There are not more than twelve or fifteen persons living here at present.

---

* From notes furnished by Dr. W. J. Hoffman.

COLUMBUS DISTRICT, NEVADA.*

The town of Columbus is situated on the southern slope of the mountains, facing the desert. Columbus district was formed and organized in December, 1864. The nearest railroad station is Wadsworth, which is one hundred and thirty-three miles distant. The district is twenty miles square. The general course of the mountains is east and west, with small spurs running off in northerly and southerly directions. The mines are located all over the mountains. The metal-bearing veins run northwest and southeast, and are found in limestone, slate, and granite. Wood occurs in abundance eight miles from town. Water is scarce, as it is taken from wells. There are three mills at this place, two of which are 5-stamps each, and one a 4-stamp mill. There is no Stedefeldt furnace attached to any of them. The ore is chiefly chloro-bromide, (embolite,) and the mills since starting, a year ago, have yielded about $30,000. Ores are worked by the dry process. The total number of tons worked is between 3,000 and 4,000. Cost of mining is $10 per ton; cost of roasting and milling, $45 per ton; cost of labor per day, at mines and mills, $4; cost of barley, 5¼ to 6 cents per pound; cost of hay, $45 per ton.

The stage runs to and from Reno; fare, $50. Freight is taken to and from Wadsworth, and costs from 4 cents to 5 cents per pound. The two 5-stamp mills work each about six tons of ore per day, and the 4-stamp mill about five tons per day, making a total of seventeen tons per diem.

The principal mines of the district are the Mount Diablo, Black, Metallic, Columbia, Northern Bell, Pèru, Potosi, Bellmarte, Pappinaux, and Vulture. Development of Mount Diablo has cost $40,000, the remaining ones each $15,000. There are five hundred or six hundred locations in the district. Total number of inhabitants about three hundred; number of houses about forty-five, including stores; stores, 4; livery stables, 2; saloons, (about,) 10.

ONEATA DISTRICT, CALIFORNIA.*

This district was formed in June, 1870. The town is ten miles from the district. Reno is one hundred and twenty-five miles from Benton and the nearest railroad station. The mines and district are located on the western slope in the northern spur of the White Mountain Range. The ore is, in appearance, a mere deposit, and the 100 tons that are now in sight yield, or are worth, according to assay, from $25,000 to $30,000.

There is running water and plenty of timber all through this part of the mountains. The ores accompany talcose slate, granite, and metamorphic limestone. The ores are all sent to Columbus for milling. Cost of working mines, $60 per ton; cost of milling, $60 per ton; cost of mining and milling labor, each $4 per day; hay worth $40 to $45 per ton.

The principal mines are the Wetherell and Indian Queen, and proceeds for one month's work (of ore) was $500. Freight to Reno is 7 cents per pound, and for ores $60 per ton. There is a 10-stamp mill and Stedefeldt furnace building now at Partzwick, costing $25,000. In these mines there are generally from twenty to thirty men employed.

MONTGOMERY DISTRICT, CALIFORNIA.*

The next district is the Montgomery, organized in 1863 by Henry B. Rich as recorder. The mountains, as in the last district, run north and south, and the mines are located over nearly all parts.

The true metalliferous veins run irregularly north and south. There is plenty of wood and water in the mountains. The rock overlying the silver-bearing rock is limestone, over which comes granite. The ore yields generally from $250 to $300 per ton. Cost of mining, per ton, $75; cost of milling, per ton, $50; cost of roasting, per ton, $15; cost of labor, per diem, $4.

SILVER PEAK AND RED MOUNTAIN MINING DISTRICTS, NEVADA.†

These mines are situated in Esmeralda County, Nevada.

Red Mountain district.—The mines in the district were discovered January 26, 1864.

Silver Peak district.—The mines in this district were discovered, and district organized February 1, 1865. The distance from railroad is one hundred and sixty miles by wagon-road. Nearest station on railroad is Wadsworth.

Timber.—This is located on the summit and west slopes of the Red Mountains, extending twelve or fifteen miles along the summit, and about ten miles from the mill. The timber-belt is about eight or ten miles wide. Varieties; Piñon or nut-pine, cedar, mountain mahogany. The timber is small, but good for that country, and plenty of it.

Water.—In Clayton Valley, near foot of eastern slope, is a cluster of large springs. They are all brackish, one or two boiling, nearly all warm, and a few cold. Water is abundant enough to run a 200-stamp mill. Also springs on west slope. Red Mountain Spring, the principal one, issues from the foot of the peak of that name. This water is pure

---

* From notes furnished by W. J. Hoffman.
† From notes furnished by Lieutenant D. A. Lyle.

and good. Limestone spring flows at least 6,000 gallons in 12 hours. Several springs on the western slope; one small alkali spring on eastern slope, about six miles from those in valley; water quite cold.

Rocks and minerals.—Limestone, granite, mica, greenstone trap; one very remarkable dike of the latter on east slope, almost vertical, about 8 feet or 10 feet thick, running from base to top, dividing the ridge into equal parts. The greenstone is eroded considerably, leaving a steeply-inclined channel through the limestone and granite, basalt. obsidian, trachytes, lava, scoria, volcanic ashes, salt, calcareous tufa, quartz, (all three varieties,) vitreous, chalcedonic, and jaspery formations, and pumice. Small crystals of smoky quartz were abundantly found in the felspathic lavas. In Clayton Valley are found trilobites, fossil fish, corals, and concretions.

Ores.—Gold—free gold in quartz and sulphurets, and auriferous galena. These have been worked by free process and wet-crushing process—amalgamated on electro-plated copper. Average yield per ton, $28. Silver—chlorides, sulphurets, argentiferous galena, and horn silver. These ores were worked awhile by the wet process, but it was a failure, yielding about 40 per cent. of the assay value. The ores of the Lodi and Tiger mines were worked successfully by the wet process, yielding 80 per cent. of assay value.

Bullion.—The gross annual production of bullion from these mines, while the mill was running, was between $900,000 and $1,000,000, averaging about $25,000 per month.

Cost of mining, milling, &c.—Average cost per ton for mining, (gold and silver mixed,) $5 per ton. (*Note.*—Perhaps a little more for gold, and a little less for silver.) Average cost for milling per ton, (no silver milled,) $3.50 for gold. Average cost for roasting, (none roasted here, some silver sent away and roasted.) Average cost for mining labor, $4 per diem. Indian labor, (used at mill,) 50 cents per diem. Cost of 10-stamp mill, (put up,) gold, $15,000; cost of 10-stamp mill, (put up,) silver, $20,000 to $25,000; cost of 20-stamp mill, (put up,) gold, $25,000; cost of 20-stamp mill, (put up,) silver, $30,000; cost of 30-stamp mill, (put up,) gold, $30,000; cost of 30-stamp mill, (put up,) silver, $50,000.

Mines worked.—The principal work has been upon the Crowning Glory Mine. The company employed seventy-five men upon it for three years at $4 per diem. The amount expended in the mineral development of these mines is about $280,000. Total amount of bullion extracted, about $2,000,000. The ore is hauled about seven or eight miles over a good road to the mill. The ore is transported down from the mine for some distance in ore-carts, over a railroad; these cars descend under the action of the force of gravity almost, and are hauled up empty by mules.

Inhabitants.—At present only four or five men remain here, all the hands having left, while the mill lies idle for repairs, and all work is suspended. There are in the place about twenty houses built of concrete, one store, and one livery stable. Materials for making concrete are close at hand, gravel being on the ground and limestone in a butte near by, and a lime-kiln near the mill. The company burn their own lime. There is one stage-line to Aurora, fare $25 to that point and $50 to Reno on railroad. Freight, 4½ cents per pound to Wadsworth. Mails weekly, I think.

DEEP SPRING VALLEY DISTRICT, CALIFORNIA.[*]

This district was organized in 1862, and called White Mountain district, but has since been changed to the above name. Nearest station on Central Pacific Railroad is Wadsworth, distance one hundred and eighty miles.

Principal Mines.

1. *Cinderella.*—This vein dips to west 5°. It is not worked now. Some miners sunk a shaft to some depth a few years ago, but were killed or driven away by the Indians. Assay value per ton, $75.

2. *San Juan.*—There has been expended in opening this mine about $2,000. It has produced so far $1,500 in bullion.

3. *Julia Dean.*—One thousand dollars have been expended on this mine. No bullion produced. Vein vertical.

4. *San Francisco.*—Five hundred dollars expended opening it.   Three hundred and sixty dollars produced in bullion.

5. *Tennant.*—One thousand dollars expended on it. Produced $500 or $600 in bullion.

6. *Homestead.*—Five hundred expended. Produced $600 in bullion.

Ores.—All silver. Some of the veins contain 33⅓ per cent. of gold, and others more. The ores must be reduced by roasting. Average yield per ton, $100. The ledges and veins are situated in both the foot-hills and main range of the White Mountains. They lie in Deep Spring Valley, in the eastern slope of those mountains, and extend from the low foot-hills to the summit. There are two systems of veins running nearly at right angles to each other. In the foot-hills the strike of the lodes is north and south. Near the summit it is nearly east and west. Country rock is granite in the foot-hills, and higher up it is talcose slate.

---

[*] From notes furnished by Mr. F. Klett.

7

Timber.—About three miles (north) in the mountains there is plenty of wood—cedar, and nut-pine. About twelve miles up on the range good pine is found.

Water.—Wyoming Creek, having its source in the mountains to the north and northwest, descending, runs southeast for four or five miles in Deep Spring Valley, and sinks in the sand; water, pure and excellent, sufficient for a small mill, at least.

Mills.—One mill here, 5-stamp battery, run by water-power, 2 pans, 1 settler, and 1 furnace; cost about $10,000. Can mill about 4 tons of ore per day.

Cost of labor.—Average cost per ton for mining the ore, $20; average cost per ton for milling and roasting, $50; mining labor per diem, $4; milling labor per diem, $3.

FISH SPRING DISTRICT, CALIFORNIA.*

This district lies in the foot-hills on the eastern side of the Sierra Nevada, about nineteen miles north of Camp Independence, California, in Owen's River Valley. The mines are small gold mines, mostly owned by one man, and worked by means of arrastras run by water-power. They yield a small but certain income. Water very abundant and excellent. My notes on this district are not at hand, which precludes any attempt at giving yields, &c.

KEARSARGE DISTRICT, CALIFORNIA.

This district is situated well up in the foot-hills of the eastern slope of the Sierras, at a distance of eight miles from Camp Independence, California. The mines are well opened at two levels, and show in each large quantities of average milling ore, that yields a good percentage and return by the well-known Washoe process. A tramway down a steep incline carries the ore from the mine to the mill, which is compactly constructed, of ten stamps, with all the modern improvements. The application of water as the power for driving the machinery is by far the prettiest specimen of the kind that I have ever seen. A mountain creek is tapped 150 feet above the mill, and the water brought in an open ditch to a plane inclined at an angle of about 40°, down which it passes with tremendous velocity until it is received by a 13½-inch turbine wheel, which it sets in motion, and which takes the part of an expensive engine in the ordinary mills.

The ores are of chloride and sulphide of silver associated with oxide, sulphide, and carbonate of lead. Many specimens are covered with crystals of molybdate of lead, and are of a yellowish-brown color. All the mines that are worked in this district belong to the Kearsarge Mining Company; they are 13 in number, and are all supposed to belong to one large fissure vein.

This is one of the many districts that would be tapped and supplied by a railroad passing to the southward from either Truckee or Wadsworth, on the Central Pacific Railroad, to the Colorado River.

SAN CARLOS DISTRICT, CALIFORNIA.

The mines are situated in the low hills nearly east from the little town of Independence, and were abandoned at the time of the burning of the mill by the Indians in 1864. It is understood that the mill is to be rebuilt and mining developments to be resumed.

LONE PINE DISTRICT, CALIFORNIA.

The mines of this district are at the little camp known as Cerro Gordo, and are principally of argentiferous galena. They were discovered some six or seven years ago, and several unsuccessful attempts made to extricate the silver lead bars from the ore, but without success; finally the process was discovered. The programme of working is now somewhat as follows: a scorifying furnace is charged with two-thirds lead ore and one-third silver ore of a poor quality, found on the eastern slope of the hills and heavily stained with carbonate of copper; this and the proper amount of charcoal is kept in a state of fusion for eight hours, then drawn off and cooled; after which it is

* From notes furnished by Lieutenant D. A. Lyle.

introduced into the ordinary blast furnace, with the requisite amounts of charcoal and salt. This system works admirably, and now enormous returns are secured from these very inaccessible mines. The ore averages from $50 to $65 per ton, in silver, the resulting bars from $260 to $300 per ton. The veins are wide, and the ore occurring in large lenticular-shaped masses trending to the southward; so far as known the supply is inexhaustible.

Notwitstanding the expensive freights, the mines are made very remunerative. The cost of transportation to Los Angeles, California, is $55 per ton; thence to San Francisco $20 per ton; thence by Pacific Mail Steamship Company to Newark, New Jersey, at an additional expense of $25 per ton.

It was found to be more profitable on account of the higher percentage of silver from the bullion, and the increased price obtained for the lead to ship to Newark, paying the extra expense, rather than to have the refining done in San Francisco.

This is only one proof out a number that can be cited, showing the advantage of large establishments where skilled labor can be concentrated, by means of which a still higher and higher percentage can be extracted from rebellious ores, which is a matter of so great necessity, especially in ores of low grade. There are three furnaces smelting ores from three mines, two at Cerro Gordo and one at Swansea, on the northern shore of Owen's Lake.

COSO DISTRICT, CALIFORNIA.

This district, situated south and east from Owen's Lake, in the Coso Range, has been worked at fitful intervals in a rude and simple manner. The quartz is gold-bearing. One of the members of the expedition found about seventy-five persons employed here, mostly Mexicans, who make use of the arrastra process for the extraction of the bullion. The fact that Americans have not occupied this ground may argue in favor of the poverty of the veins, which, added to the presence of the surrounding desert on three sides, make the locality anything but an inviting one.

GRANITE MOUNTAIN DISTRICT, CALIFORNIA.*

The mines of this district were discovered by Mr. Egan, of Swansea, and the district organized a year or so ago.

Principal mines.—The principal mines are situated on the west side of Granite Mountain, a high abrupt peak in the Tortoise Range, and are at a great altitude. The principal mines are the Toronto, Santa Clara, and Alta. The bluffs in which they are situated are very steep and almost vertical, and to the south of Santa Clara is a trapdike, nearly vertical, cutting the strata. Country rock—granite, limestone, and metamorphic slate. The ledges of mineral are near the juncture of the strata of slate and lime. The ores are galena, associated with some carbonate of lead, with quartz; a good deal of hard limestone is interstratified with the galena.

The Alta is above the Santa Clara, and has a mineral vein several feet wide; hematitic iron was found in this vein; also, perhaps, a little magnetite; but the Santa Clara is the chief lode; this is an immense bed of mineral, and is apparently quite rich; the metalliferous vein is many feet thick, and, perhaps, extends through to the eastern side of the peak in a horizontal direction.

Timber.—There is little or none in the immediate vicinity of the mines, but ten or fifteen miles distant along the range, plenty for fuel is found.

Water.—Plenty of water is found in Darwin Cañon, a very narrow and contracted gorge cut through slate; this is about two or three miles from the mines.

Communication.—A road could be built from Owen's Lake to Darwin Cañon, but sand would be very deep in places; considerable labor would be required at others. A trail leads from the cañon up to the mines, a good one, but very steep. It is said that a road can be built up another cañon to the south and southwest of mines, to within a mile at the farthest. I did not pass over this ground, but think, from what I saw of the termini, it would cost considerable, both in labor and money, and the ore would then have to be packed down on mules to the road, for some time at least after the mines are worked. The mines are not worked yet.

---

* From notes furnished by Lieutenant D. A. Lyle.

TELESCOPE DISTRICT, CALIFORNIA.

Visited by a topographical party. (No notes.) Situated south and west from Telescope Peak; deserted at the time of our visit for want of means on the part of the owners to prosecute explorations.

LYONS DISTRICT, CALIFORNIA.

Discovered in 1871. Lies in Cottonwood Cañon, that runs into the northwestern arm of Death Valley. The veins are true fissures of low-grade ore, protruding through solid granite near where eruptive beds of volcanic rock have come in. A fine stream of water rises near the head of the cañon, and sinks after flowing three or four miles. This is fringed along its entire length with heavy cottonwoods. This locality has been but little prospected, but undoubtedly is mineral-bearing over quite a large area.

DEATH VALLEY DISTRICT, CALIFORNIA.

This district, as its name indicates, overlooks the valley of that name, being on the eastern slope of the Telescope Range. A little mining for gold from quartz was done here. The same remarks apply as in the case of the Telescope District.

EL PASO DISTRICT, CALIFORNIA.*

This district lies twenty-eight miles southeast of Walker's Pass, or about one hundred and seventy-five miles from Los Angeles or Visalia, and is easily accessible, over fair roads. Timber none. Excellent water may be had from wells. Formation, of easily decomposing granite, associated with metamorphic rocks, and carrying quartz and felspar seams. The quartz seems to contain mostly sulphides and chlorides. Iron and copper pyrites are present, considerable argentiferous galena, and silver and lead ores. Three adits have been started and several shafts, the deepest being abou t 50 feet. The main adit had been driven about 100 feet in a S. 25° E. direction, with an inclination of about 8°. I found no seams exposed in the openings, finding specimens only in the dump and in some unopened seams, which looked as if perhaps workable. The mining was evidently of the simplest description. Mines at present entirely deserted.

AMARGOSA MINES, CALIFORNIA.*

Twenty miles east of the south end of Death Valley, and north of Camp Cady, near the old Mormon trail. They are deserted, though the remains of buildings, adits, and stump-heads, &c., show that considerable work has been done. Wood and grass entirely wanting, while the little water present is very alkaline. The adits are in granite, run at random in from the sides of a cañon; they follow no seams, veins, or deposits of any kind, and none could be found, while there was no ore discoverable in the dump-piles or *débris*. The distance from the base of supplies, and the desert nature of the country, would prohibit anything but the very richest of mines to be worked with any profit.

TIMBER MOUNTAIN DISTRICT, NEVADA.

Discovered in 1869, in Spring Mountain Range, north and west from Las Vegas ranch. The ores are galena and sulphide of silver, in addition to large deposits of low-grade base metal silver ores, distributed over a large area. The high mountains are heavily wooded. All the appurtenances for mining can easily be rendered available, and the Colorado River will, in time, be the outlet for these ores.

YELLOW PINE DISTRICT, NEVADA.†

The mine is on the crest of a fractured anticlinal of limestone of Carboniferous age. The broken strata make with each other an angle of 90°, and have received little, if any, relative vertical displacement along the plane of fracture. Supposing, as is presumable, that the fracture has afforded a channel for the distribution of the ores, it is probable that other bodies, similar to those already found, are irregularly disposed among the crushed beds below, but a continuous lead is not to be anticipated.

---

* From notes furnished by Mr. A. R. Marvine.
† From notes furnished by Mr. G. K. Gilbert.

The Comet mine was the only one visited in this district, and it is understood to be the prominent mine. The ore is of the smelting order, but, judging from general appearances, does not carry, as a matrix constituent, a natural flux. Should such be the case, this mine cannot be worked with profit, since the present remote location will not permit of transporting to the site of the mine an artificial fluxing agent. I quite agree with Mr. Gilbert as regards his notions of permanency, from a common experience among limestone districts. Galena ores, as a rule, are deposits in beds or pockets, rather than as veins. The Yellow Pine district as organized, however, is of great extent, and is said to show a multiplicity of locations and ores. Doubtless many of them will be utilized, and the Colorado River act as the channel of shipment, as these mountains offer favorable facilities, such as water, grass, wood, and timber, for mining. The main portion of the range has an exposure of lime-stone, overlaid at certain localities near the center of this district by quartzite, and along its northeastern slopes by eruptive beds of volcanic rock. There is an immense body of heavy pine timber distributed over a great share of the higher elevations of the Spring Mountain Range.

CLARKE DISTRICT.

This district is situated partly in Nevada and partly in California. The first reduction from the field notes places Ivanpah and the mines in its immediate vicinity in Nevada, while those farther to the south are in California. This result should not, however, be considered as final, since it is subject to certain sources of error.

The mines here are in three groups, and show entirely dissimilar characteristics. The most northerly groups, in the vicinity of Ivanpah, occur as thin veins in limestone, and dipping out from the hill where opened. Ores rich, showing stromeyerite and stedefeldtite, and some chloride of silver. The pay-streak is very narrow; the country rock greatly disturbed.

The more southern locations were not visited. The first lot found in the vicinity of Clarke Mountain occur in granite, and are reported as wide veins of low-grade silver.

Still farther south, nearly fifteen miles, large deposits of copper have been located, and opened to some extent. Water is scarce in the northern part, but more plenty lower down the range. The country offers natural facilities for mining, and Cottonwood Island, on the Colorado, can be reached by an easy grade.

The want of capital, here as elsewhere, is sadly noticed. The mines are numerous, and in the hands of a well-organized and powerful company ought to be made remunerative.

Contracts were in operation for building a 5-stamp mill at Ivanpah; this would render available considerable ore now on the dumps, valued at about $100 per ton. Ore at present is shipped on a small scale, via Los Angeles, three hundred and seventy-five miles, to San Francisco for reduction. Mining labor, $3 per day. Indian labor is utilized to a small extent. Freight from Los Angeles is 6 cents per pound. No indications of water in any of the shafts; but a well is being sunk between the mines and the town and on the western slope of the range. Depth, 70 feet; no water so far.

NEW YORK DISTRICT, NEVADA AND CALIFORNIA.

This district lies south and east from Clarke Mountain, at a distance of seventeen miles. Mines extend on the western side of the range. Deposits of a cupreous sort of ore were noticed, probably very poor in silver. Galena and sulphuret ores were found on the eastern slope. Water scarce, wood and grass plenty. Approaches to the Colorado River easy.

HUALAPAIS DISTRICT, ARIZONA.

This was located years ago, and known as the Sacramento district. Some labor was spent, with little success, until finally the parties were driven out by Indians.

In the spring of 1871 a party of prospectors re-entered the district, and discovered many new veins, showing almost every variety of silver ores. Some little excitement followed, and very many claims were located. The general direction of the ledges is from north 40° west, to north 55° west, and the surface exposure of mineral is the largest I have ever seen. The veins occur in solid granite, and along edges of eruptive volcanic beds, and are wide and well defined. Many of the surface ores are rich, and especially the narrow veins, most of which will prove to be feeders. Both gold and silver are found, the latter predominating. The veins that are to be permanent will be of the lower-grade ores, but yet of sufficient richness to admit of their being worked even in this locality. There are evidences that the water-level is to be found early, and that the ore will assume a more permanent form, principally of the blue sulphuret variety. One of the handsomest veins that it has ever been my fortune to examine was the Porter mine, at that time the best developed in depth in the district, showing a distinctly organized vein in solid granite at 55 feet. Mining operations can now be conducted in the northwestern part of Arizona, as the Hualapais Indians, occupying this section, have been subdued and are at peace. The Colorado River is near at hand as a mode of transit, and the projected Atlantic and Pacific Railroad passes midway between several mining districts that border on the river. I look upon this district as one of the most promising in Arizona, and, indeed, among many of those met in my travels. One 5-stamp, free process mill is in process of erection.

MAYNARD DISTRICT, ARIZONA.

This district was discovered in 1871, and lies on the eastern slope of the Hualapais Mountains at a distance of thirty miles from the Needles on the Colorado River, and the railroad near the thirty-fifth parallel passes within nine miles of the principal locations. The mineral belt covers an area of nearly twenty square miles. The veins are similar to those in the Hualapais district, have the same direction, and, in fact, to a remarkable degree, these districts are counterparts No work done yet. Wood, timber, and water are plenty. The site for a mining-camp is very desirable. This locality also will act as a center, from which much prospecting will be done further down the same range; also to the south and east, and bordering the country of the Apache-Mohaves, from which locality float-mineral was noticed in different places.

The mines in the vicinity of Prescott were visited by Lieutenant Lockwood, and a slight memorandum appears in his report.

Those about Bradshaw Mountains were visited by a party under Lieutenant Lyle, and his remarks are quoted. Later statistical information has been obtained from this locality, which is to be collated in systematic form for a subsequent report. From very many localities during the season float-mineral has been brought into camp, until one is weary with so much mineral and so many mountains. It all adds to that forcible proof, already established in my own mind, that the stores of precious minerals in our western territory are inexhaustible, and that mining in the United States is only in its infancy.

MINES IN BRADSHAW MOUNTAINS, ARIZONA.*

These mines lie southeast from Prescott, Arizona Territory, and about forty miles distant. The principal mining districts are the Tiger, Pine Grove, and Bradshaw, in the Bradshaw Mountains, and near Bradshaw City, a mining-camp near the summit of the mountain and at an elevation of about 7,000 feet. These mines are on the main range of mountains, whose trend is nearly north and south.

TIGER DISTRICT, ARIZONA.*

This district was organized in June, 1871, by the Tiger Mining Company. Principal mines: Tiger, California, Benton, Gray Eagle, Loreno, and Eclipse. There are several other ledges, but these are the principal ones.

* From notes furnished by Lieutenant D. A. Lyle.

1. *Tiger.*—This mine is opened by a shaft 90 feet deep, and a level run 20 feet below the surface, and another one at the depth of 80 feet. Country rock: granite and slate. The hanging and foot walls are, both of them, slate in all the mines in the Tiger district. Croppings bold. Ores: sulphurets of silver; assays $800 to $1,000 per ton, first-class ore; $60 to $80 general average; width of vein, 10 feet. The vein has been traced for four or five miles.

2. *California.*—Ledge 30 feet thick, and two miles long. Ores: silver; chlorides and sulphurets; all the mines in the district, silver with a little gold.

PINE GROVE DISTRICT, ARIZONA.*

This district was organized in June, 1870. Principal mines: Blandina, Moreland, New Era, Shelton, and Hunter. Ores: gold and silver; sulphurets and chlorides. Course of veins, north and south, northeast and southwest. No work being done yet.

BRADSHAW DISTRICT, ARIZONIA.*

Date of organization unknown, but prior to the others. Principal mines: Del Pasco, War Eagle, and Bradshaw. Ores: gold-quartz; course of veins, north and south and northeast and southwest; country rock: granite; foot-walls: granite and sometimes the hanging-walls. Timber: plenty of pine, juniper, and some oak. Building and mining timber is abundant on the ground and excellent in quality. Water: scarce—not enough for milling purposes. It is found in the shafts, but it is questionable whether the supply will be sufficient for mining purposes. Mills: no mill or machinery yet in the Tiger district; a small 5-stamp gold-mill in Bradshaw district for milling rock taken from the Del Pasco mine; water supply not very abundant. Cost of various articles at Bradshaw City: hay, per ton, $75; barley, per pound, 15 cents; lumber, per thousand feet, $100; miners, $2.50 per day and board; blasting-powder, per keg, $15; freight, per pound, 15 cents; cost of a 5-stamp mill, (put up,) $10,000; cost of a 10-stamp mill, $15,000 to $20,000; cost of a 20-stamp mill, $25,000.

Remarks.—Prescott, Arizona Territory, is the nearest post-office, about forty miles distant, reached by a trail. This has a good track, but is, in many places, very steep. There is a wagon-road from Walnut Grove to Minnehaha Flat, five miles from Bradshaw City. A steep trail leads up from the flat to the city. The place contains about one dozen log-houses and a store.

TURKEY CREEK DISTRICT, ARIZONA.*

Mines are deserted; they are all gold, I think; an old dismantled mill on Turkey Creek; lack of water for mining purposes.

WEAVER DISTRICT, ARIZONA.*

This district is situated south of Antelope Mountain and in the vicinity of Wickenburg, Arizona Territory. Recorder, C. P. Stanton, at Vulture City, three and one-fourth miles north of Wickenburg. Principal mines: Great Sexton and Mason.

1. *Great Sexton.*—This mine is opened by a shaft and tunnel. Ores: gold-bearing quartz; assays $30 per ton. Only fifty tons have been worked at Vulture mill; result not known.

2. *Mason.*—Opened by a shaft; ore worked by horse arrastras. Ores: gold and silver, with quartz; assays $640 silver and $27 gold per ton. Country rock: quartz and granite. General course of veins in district: northeast and southwest.

Mills, cost of labor, &c.—Vulture mill, at Vulture City, is a 40-stamp mill. Mining-labor, $3 to $4 per day. Wood, at Vulture City, $10 per cord; very scarce. Plenty of grass and water.

WALNTUT GROVE DISTRICT, ARIZONA.*

None of the veins are being worked now in this district; no water for past two seasons. Principal mines: Sutler, Blue Jay, Big Rebel, Josephine, Robinson, and Crescent Lead.

1. *Sutler.*—Ores refractory; both gold and silver found, but principally gold; assays $30 gold, $17 to $18 silver per ton; no galena; thickness of lode, 22 feet pay-ore; course of vein, northeast and southwest.

2. *Blue Jay.*—This mine was opened by a shaft and tunnel, the latter 70 feet in length, run on a 4-foot vein of gold and silver.

3. *Big Rebel.*—Opened by a tunnel; gold-bearing quartz in slate formation; lode 12 feet thick; course of vein, northeast and southwest; assays $37 gold per ton.

---

* From notes furnished by Lieutenant D. A. Lyle.

4. *Josephine.*—Opened by a tunnel in years 1865 and 1866; vein in slate; 18 inches thick of pay-rock; course of lode, north and south; assays $47 per ton; contains some free gold.

5. *Robinson.*—Opened by a shaft and tunnel, the tunnel tapping the vein 80 feet below the surface; course of lodes north and south; ores quite rich; $90 to $100 per ton resulting from working arrastras; free gold. It is said that a mill will soon be erected for working this mine.

6. *Crescent Lead.*—Ore, galena; assays $884 silver, and 62 per cent. of lead; 5 feet of pure metal; course of lode, northeast and southwest; no work done yet.

Remark.—All these mines held by miners under United States laws.

HASSYAMPA DISTRICT, ARIZONA.*

The Montgomery is the principal mine, located in October, 1863; worked by horse-arrastras; $250 to $300, free gold, resulting; have had no water now for two years. This was the first mine opened in Yavapais County, Arizona Territory.

MARTINEZ DISTRICT, ARIZONA.*

The mines in this district lie south and southwest from Camp Date Creek. Principal mines: Mayflower and Martinez.

1. *Mayflower.*—Mine, gold; matrix matter, quartz; country rock, granite; strike of lode, northeast and southwest; opened by a shaft sunk 40 feet; $10,000 expended on this mine; ore hauled to Vulture mill, twenty miles distant; water scarce—some in Martinez Creek, two miles distant; course of creek, southeast—empties into Hassyampa.

2. *Martinez.*—This mine is said to be richer than the Mayflower; gold-quartz, formerly worked by arrastras; first ton paid $129 gold; not working now; cost of mining-labor, $3 to $4 per day. Title, miner's: these two mines are nearly south of Camp Date Creek, Arizona Territory, and six miles distant.

SANTA MARIA DISTRICT, ARIZONA.*

Boundaries unknown; the Rhinoceros is the principal mine; lode 3 feet thick, inclosed in walls nearly vertical; not working now.

VULTURE MINE, ARIZONA.

This mine, so noted as being famous among the gold mines of Arizona, could not be visited this summer for want of time; however, certain information has been gathered, which will be placed in form in due time. One point of significance is the fact that at the mine it is reported that there are more than 1,000,000 tons of ore, of low grade, that cannot be transported 14 miles to the mill, for reduction, because of the cost. The dump-piles at a great many mines all over the country are groaning with just such loads as this; certainly an argument in favor of concentrating processes, and increased and cheapened facilities for mining. In this connection let me say that I believe that the production of gold from Arizona is likely to be far in advance of the same mineral from Nevada. The mines in Apache Pass, visited in 1868, are somewhat similar in character to the Vulture mine, and are sure to become productive upon the opening up of the country.

MINES IN THE PINAL MOUNTAINS, ARIZONA.

Upon reaching Tucson it was found that considerable interest was evinced in some late discoveries in the Pinal Mountains, a pretty dangerous Indian locality. Notice of these will be found in Lieutenant Lockwood's report, and the following remarks of Dr. Hoffman are herewith attached:

Gold.—Auriferous sand was found near the trail leading from the Salt River to Camp Pinal, about eight miles south of the river. The formation was syenitic, with occasional bowlders of granite. Minute particles of gold were visible in the sand, and specimens, or rather samples, of sand preserved. *Note.*—It is believed that prospectors so far have been unsuccessful in utilizing these same placers.

---

* From notes furnished by Lieutenant D. A. Lyle.

Silver.—On nearing Camp Pinal, and about six miles north, we found float, (in the different washes,) consisting of stromeyerites, with their coatings of azurite and malachite. The fragments were rich, and would probably be worth $100 to $150 per ton; but these were, apparently, choice pieces. The float was found on both the northern and southern slopes of the Pinal Mountains. After we arrived at Florence, I saw members of a private prospecting party, who had fine specimens of silver ore, and which they claimed upon assay was worth $7,000 per ton. I think it utterly impossible, as the ore consisted of a cupreous and argentiferous hematite, with blotches of stromeyerite, &c.

Until the Indian difficulty is settled, mining must remain practically at a stand-still in Arizona, except in the northwest part of the Territory and certain other strips that border the Colorado River.

In closing this subject, which somewhat in detail has given the frame-work of what may be considered as worthy of receiving attention on the part of Government explorations, a few suggestions will be ventured upon material, though not new, yet that still has a vital bearing upon the mining interests of the far West, that are slowly struggling toward their merited prominence, and upon subjects worthy the attention of our political economists and legislators.

The time is fast approaching when the mining interest is to assume a greater national promise and the one, next to agriculture, that calls for an enlightened support on the part of the Government.

Experience, already gained, leads to the conclusion that it is proper, as among the first steps, to set apart certain areas from the public domain, to be segregated from the public lands and to be known as "mineral lands," to be subject to entry, patent, and sale as such, and governed by special laws, the details of which have been so selected that the Government interests shall be secured, that free and equal rights to all the miners shall be obtained, so that the public lands, held in heritage for succeeding generations, shall not be created into a subsidy to the mineral interest, and so that a fresh impetus shall be given to mining enterprises that are to depend upon our private capital legitimately employed for their support. From the mapping out of the geographical boundaries of various districts it appears that they often overlap each other and follow no standard regarding size, therefore early legislation may well fix these limits that surround any specially discovered mineral area, and as the longer axis of the mineral cropping is generally sensibly north and south, the limiting rectangle might well be established to not exceed twenty miles in this direction, and fourteen miles in an easterly and westerly direction, measuring from the central location. So far as segregating areas of land from the public lands and applying them to mineral purposes is concerned, it cannot result in detriment to the Government interests, that accrue from the occupation and sale of new lands. Since the laws governing the new disposition have for their precedent the system that has worked so admirably in securing homesteads to settlers in remote sections, and stipulate similar terms, but away from the sea-board, from close inland transportation, the interior mining districts, of which the number increases year by year, need all that surrounds them to themselves, as a part and parcel of their own integral character. Furthermore, at ninety-nine out of every one hundred districts, agricultural land as such has no marketable value unless the mines are worked, and the remunerations from mining enterprises are not generally so great as to render it advisable for a capitalist to seek a remote corner where mines are for sale and first purchase a shaky possessory title to a mine, successively titles to water, mill, wood sites and other necessary conveniences for conducting his operations. It seems highly desirable that this idea of setting aside mineral districts as such should be favorably considered.

The local mining laws in districts that are distant from settlements are generally formed by the parties of prospectors who push out in advance, and, discovering fresh mineral, at once set out to form a district. Ordinarily these parties have no text at hand that gives them a version of

8

the best known local mining laws, and are probably unskilled in legal or other technicalities; they create a system of laws which would answer very well if the mines were of no value, but in case of sudden developments of wealth, where chances to question the validity or extent of a claim are involved, the loose description from the records affords one of the arguments in favor of litigation. Therefore, it seems not unwise to frame a set of local mining laws that shall be generally acceptable to all the interests involved, that branch out into new and unprospected regions, and which shall conform to the United States laws already enacted and which shall be accessible to all. The nearest approach to such a system was found in the set of by-laws adopted to control the Blind Mountain district, that were prepared by an able mining lawyer in San Francisco, whose long experience entitles him to consideration.

They would be quoted here only that the space does not permit. On the part of Congress, the most earnest solicitude should be evinced to so amend the general mining law, from time to time, as to make it conform to the strict sense of needs that are requisite to the various mining sections, to be governed by experience and knowledge gathered from time to time from reliable sources.

It is believed that the bill now before the mining committee in Congress has stipulations defining, with a greater accuracy and with a more liberal tone, the limits and integral character of a "vein, lode, ledge, or deposit," and embraces details favorable to a more speedy method of obtaining a secure title to mineral property.

By persons whose experience has led them to take a comprehensive view of the wants of the mineral interest in our western territory, and to the position that the Government should assume as the guardian of this trust, the necessity and desirability of a national school of mines has already been urged. For me to concur would be only to reiterate ideas already advanced; presuming, then, upon the use and practicability, it only remains to mark the place, and the single suggestion offered is, that it should be at Washington. Besides, it may be urged as a national economy that the proceeds available from the sale of mineral lands should be devoted to the maintenance of such an institution.

One of the urgent wants felt in the promotion of our mining industry is that of increased and cheapened inland transportation. River transportation upon our western coast is, to a great extent, a failure, as beyond the Columbia and Colorado Rivers, that furnish somewhat irregular avenues of connection with the interior, no streams of considerable magnitude exist; river transportation, even in this very American age, loses its great power when pitted against railroads, as instanced at many localities in the valley of the Mississippi, where railroads supersede the river modes of transportation because of speed and time.

Therefore, it is railroads that the mining interiors of the western coast need, and it is not believed that Congress should, at this season, be so sparing of its land-grants to aid private capital in the prosecution of these schemes, since, having already given over to private corporations the better share of the lands that yet remain, there is relatively but little danger of diminishing the prospective revenue of the country by withholding from corporations, devoted to local interests only, grants of the very inferior land that in the majority of instances will inclose these lines of road. Narrow-gauge roads, that have met with so much favor upon the Continent, and which at present are being slowly introduced in the United States, recommend themselves at once to any one desirous of seeing this character of communication brought, as speedily as possible, to the doors of our mineral wealth.

In the new areas of silver-bearing veins that are becoming so numerous, it requires but little discrimination to show that the majority of the ores are complex in their character, and that the present known methods of reduction give only an approximate percentage of their silver-bearing value; therefore, the improvements that are from time to time suggested in the methods that may be adopted for the extraction of a higher percentage of bullion, are worthy of attention. Thus it is that, on account of greater facilities of talent and machinery, the refinery at Newark is in advance of that at San Francisco, and, in turn, that of Swansea collects the best-known methods of reduction; but cannot the skill and knowledge that is aggregated at these centers be diffused again, so that we can bring to little mining camps in the interior, practical results that shall enable them to resume operation upon one that is worth twenty dollars per ton, which before must remain untouched, because impossible to obtain from it more than fifteen? A subject worthy of note, since for many years the shipment of the base-metal ores will be made to these reduction centers, is that of concentration of ores by the specific gravity or entirely mechanical process. Several attempts at this have been made, but with, so far, but little success.

The mechanical appliances are imperfect, but are susceptible to that modification that shall prove the availability of the method. The introduction of cheapened labor, and especially in remote districts, a subject so sensibly urged by Mr. R. W. Raymond, United States Commissioner of Mining Statistics, merits favorable consideration. Let this labor come from whatever quarter of the globe it may, let it be Asiatic, African, European, or American, there should be no restriction to free trade in this particular when the necessities of a national interest require it for its development. I am led to believe that one thing that hinders greatly the embarking of capital in new localities is the want of reliable information as to the presence and position of the mineral-bearing ores.

The bullion product of the country, since statistics have been collected, has been found to vary within limits never exceeding ninety millions of dollars per annum; after the exhaustion of the placer-mines of California, this product sensibly decreased, until a reaction in its favor was experienced from the early results furnished by the Comstock lode. Much prospecting has been done since that time and a great many mineral districts located; the common experience proves these to be principally of silver. The sizes and grades of the districts are varied. They are all possessed of a greater or less amount of the precious metals, and in the prosperous future are to contribute to our national wealth and necessities, so that those who live to see the close of the present century may not be surprised at an annual product of bullion as large as one hundred and fifty millions, no more than they may be at the fact of the present ore in sight in Washoe—a mine which by many was not long since thought to be practically exhausted—of a supposed value of fifteen millions of dollars; all of this, provided enlightened legislation will study and assist the want of legitimate mineral enterprises.

Silver ore occurs in connection with limestone, granite, the older volcanic rocks, as propylite, andesite, rhyolite, &c., and quartzite; the instances of the latter are, however, very rare, as among the former very numerous, although the deposits are wanting in determinate characteristics.

From the latest and most reliable geological contributions to our knowledge as to the epoch of formation of the silver-bearing veins, this period is fast being narrowed down to a much more recent geologic age than was formerly supposed.

MAPS.

The map now presented embraces in preliminary form some of the most general topographical information, the location of routes pursued, the positions of mining camps, &c. A rough transcript from most of the topographical notes of the season is given. The final map, on a scale of one inch to six miles, will delineate the topography in detail, and will be constructed with great care. Profiles of the more important north and south lines are to be produced.

[NOTE.—Information, where furnished by members of the expedition, is printed in small type.]

Contour maps of two mining districts are in process of preparation.

A skeleton map, showing the areas occupied by the Indian tribes and their reservations, will be furnished for the use of the Indian Bureau.

A statistical map, showing relative amounts of arable, mineral, and desert sections, will receive attention.

A skeleton map embracing the perimeter lines of the great interior and exterior basins of this region is to be projected.

CONCLUSION.

Although the day of the path-finder has sensibly ended in this country, still it is expected that among the results of an exploration there should be something new. In summing up the effort will be made to lay the groundwork of the new discoveries, if such they may be termed, the bearing that these may have on further and more extended explorations, and estimates for their continuance.

As a subject of primal importance, the mapping out of the mining districts already discovered, locating their positions, areas, directions of lodes, &c., determining their place as links in the great chain of mineral deposition throughout the entire Cordillera system, and as presenting limits to the field for search for the precious minerals, the result fully sustains the most sanguine anticipations, proving the existence of mineral districts over large areas, and also that the field for prospecting has only commenced, although it may have progressed somewhat in advance of the interior development of new sections of country.

The topographical features of the great Colorado plateau have been developed along that portion of its perimeter from the vicinity of Saint George, in Utah, to the White Mountains rising out of it, near the border line between Arizona and New Mexico. Geological data along new ground in that specially rich field among the lower cañons of the Colorado have been gathered. The limits, character, and relations of a number of inclosed and entirely interior basins in Nevada and Southeastern California have been determined. A further exploration of the Colorado has finally determined the absolute head of navigation, the limit beyond which a party of examination will not be likely to ascend the river, and that, although navigation, subject to many difficulties, may be carried somewhat higher than had been expected, still the wants of the interior country will not demand this above a certain specified point. It has been ascertained that a railroad can cross the Colorado at the mouth of the Virgin River and be carried along easy grades into Arizona; also, that the Colorado can be crossed by a north and south line near the foot of the Grand Cañon, and that this route may at once be made available for mails to the northern part of Arizona, and for the inland passage of troops.

The almost incredible vertical height of the walls of the Grand Cañon has been verified, as also the crater character of the San Francisco Mountains. Auriferous sand and gravel has been noted at various points on the Colorado and along the tributaries from the plateaus, and at other localities, though the rumor of rich and extensive placer deposits is discredited.

The usual number of rumors of diamonds and precious stones were heard, but it is believed that their position must now be limited to quite inaccessible portions that have not yet been visited.

Much light has been thrown upon the limits of the great interior basins and also that of the Colorado. These are a few of the subjects, sensibly new, that suggest themselves; from continued investigations of a similar nature may be expected novel and unique information upon the same and allied subjects. The first grand necessity lies in the fact that the country ought to be more thoroughly mapped, both for military and civil purposes. In order to carry out this mapping project, parties in force must repair to this field, and they ought to be liberally and systematically fitted out; and hence schemes of exploration should follow a settled plan and form a special part and parcel of the annual estimates submitted to Congress.

In this connection, there is herewith submitted for the action of the Department the basis of a plan for the surveys and explorations necessary to a complete reconstruction of the engineer map of the Western Territories, referring more especially to areas west of the one hundredth meridian of longitude. From a careful study of this map it appears that there are fully 175,000 square miles of territory unexamined instrumentally, located sensibly as follows: In Southern and Southeastern California, 25,000 square miles; in Southeastern, Eastern, Northwestern, and Western Arizona, 18,000 square miles; in Southwestern and Northern New Mexico, 15,000 square miles; in Southwestern Colorado, 10,000 square miles; in Western and Southeastern Utah, 20,000 square miles; in Northeastern Wyoming, 12,000 square miles; in Northwestern Dakota, 10,000 square miles; in Western Montana, 26,000 square miles; in Southeastern Idaho, 15,000 square miles; in Northwestern, Northern, and Northeastern Nevada, 10,000 square miles; in Southern and Southeastern Oregon, 14,000 square miles; and in Central Washington Territory, 10,000 square miles.

In advance it can scarcely be expected that a limitation as to time can be set for the prosecution to completion of this work; several seasons, however, of field and office labor will be requisite.

In view of the many interests involved, whose development may be materially improved by a continuance of these surveys, I have the honor to request the Department to call to the attention of Congress the necessity of an appropriation for the ensuing fiscal year of $75,000, founded upon the following estimate, somewhat in detail:

Pay of civilian assistants, in field	$15,400 00
Pay of civilian assistants, in office	7,300 00
Pay of guides, packers, laborers, &c., in field	15,120 00
Annual purchase of instruments	5,000 00
Annual repairs of instruments	1,000 00
Annual purchase of material and incidentals	3,500 00
Purchase of animals, and transportation accounts	10,000 00
Forage for animals	12,000 00
Contingencies	5,680 00
Total	75,000 00

The first requisite will be to establish a base line; the central line from Omaha west follows in general relations the railroad already completed, and a comprehensive system of astronomical points should be established at the most feasible and characteristic stations along this line, so that the astronomical positions may be obtained, using the telegraph; this system to be developed laterally as rapidly as the telegraph reaches interior localities. The expeditions should make their first rendezvous points along this line of road, and follow as nearly as possible north and south lines. I shall at an early date present to the Department a complete and detailed plan regarding the establishment of this astronomical base, and that field of surveys adjacent to, and which ought first to be taken up, to continue and complete investigations already begun along north and south lines.

To a person not well acquainted with the mountain interior of the Pacific coast, the grand advantage of a longitudinal view of its physical structure can scarcely be understood.

At a subsequent period the subject of the value of the surveys (in our western interior with which the Engineer Department have, from time to time, been charged) to the Executive Departments of the Government and to the industral interests of the country, will be taken up and discussed as an advance toward the idea of a survey or surveys of a more national character, which the best interests of the country, whether in war or in peace, will call for at no distant day.

APPENDIX A.

REPORT OF DANIEL W. LOCKWOOD, FIRST LIEUTENANT OF ENGINEERS.

WASHINGTON, D. C., *February* 28, 1872.

SIR: I have the honor to submit the following preliminary report with regard to operations connected with your late expedition through Nevada and Arizona, and carried on under my immediate charge, being governed by instructions received from you from time to time.

Having reported to you at Camp Independence, California, August 1, 1871, in compliance with telegraphic instructions from the commanding general, Military Division of the Pacific, dated San Francisco, California, May 16, 1871, I on the following day assumed command of main party No. 2 of your expedition, as directed by the following order:

ENGINEER'S OFFICE, EXPLORATIONS IN NEVADA AND ARIZONA,
Rendezvous Camp near Independence, California, August 2, 1871.

[Special Field Orders No. 18.]

I. Lieutenant D. W. Lockwood, Corps of Engineers, having reported at these headquarters, will assume entire and permanent charge of main party No. 2 of the expedition, for general instructions conforming to the spirit of paragraph 2 Special Orders No. 109, Adjutant General's Office, 18th of March, 1871, and the letter of the Chief of Engineers of March 23, 1871.

He will conduct this main line of the explorations along routes that will be from time to time designated to him, and while *en route* between rendezvous camps he will conduct his party precisely as if it were a separate expedition.

Besides his executive duties, he will take personal charge of sextant astronomical work, more particularly with a view to correct latitude stations.

Upon reaching Washington at the termination of the field labors of the explorations of this season, he will prepare at once a preliminary report of operations, to be followed as soon as practicable by a detailed report, accompanied by sub-reports of certain civilian assistants.

GEO. M. WHEELER,
First Lieutenant, Corps of Engineers, Commanding Expedition.

The time from August 2 to August 10 was employed in refitting, &c., and on the latter date the party left camp to proceed to Stump Springs, designated as the next point of rendezvous.

Your expedition having been in the field for several months at the time of reporting for duty, I found, upon assuming command of main party No. 2, the special organization for field-work complete, and would recommend the plan adopted by you as one particularly suited to the character of the country traversed, and the nature of the operations conducted under your charge during the past season.

The *personnel* of the party was changed, from time to time, but was always kept up in such a manner as to enable me to apply myself more particularly to duties of an administrative character and to daily astronomical work.

The departments of geology, mineralogy, and natural history were represented throughout the season, and the topographical department nearly all the time was in charge of Chief Topographer Louis Nell, who merits my full commendation for the skill and energy he displayed. The party was in the field under my charge from August 2 to December 4, 1871, and during that time traveled a distance of one thousand two hundred and eighty-nine miles *en route* from Camp

Independence, California, to Tucson, Arizona Territory, the general course being as follows: Down Owen's River Valley to Desert Wells; thence east to the Cottonwoods via the Amargosa River; from the Cottonwoods to Saint George, on the old Salt Lake road; thence south down the Grand Wash to the Ute crossing on the Colorado River. The passage of the river having been effected with the assistance of the boat parties, the Colorado plateau was followed to Truxton Springs, Arizona Territory. Leaving this point, Prescott was reached via Young's Spring and Bill Williams's Mountain, passing around its northern slope. From here the route to Tucson was via Camp Verde and Sunset Crossing on the Colorado Chiquito to Camp Apache; thence via old Camp Pinal to the place mentioned.

The main object of the expedition, as indicated in the letter of instructions from the Chief of Engineers, dated Engineer Office, Washington, D. C., March 23, 1871, being the obtaining of correct topographical knowledge of the area traversed, and its embodiment in an accurate map, the principal labors were in carrying out this requirement. The plan adopted was the same as in 1869, the different points along the route being located by triangulation with a Cassella theodolite, and the length of base line determined by odometer measurements.

The positions of camps, as determined by this method, were corrected by astronomical observations, the instruments used being sextant 2831 by Troughton and Simms, and mean solar chronometers. Whenever circumstances would permit of it, equal altitudes of the sun were taken for time, and circum-meridian altitudes of the same body for latitude. Generally, however, as the camps along the route were only for one night, east and west stars were taken for time and Polaris for latitude. By comparison of the results thus obtained with those determined at the main astronomical stations, where a transit and zenith instrument combined was used, the probable error of latitude, at least, can be reduced to a very small limit.

With regard to the topographical features of the area passed over, the changes were so frequent and so complete that no general description will suffice for the whole, and I therefore shall present this subject more in detail with regard to locality than would otherwise be necessary. Some idea, however, of the change in character of topographical features along the route traveled may be formed when the nature of the transition from the desert valleys and lofty, rugged, volcanic mountains of Southern California to the elevated plateau bordering the Colorado River, and generally Northern Arizona, is fully understood.

On the 10th of August the party left Independence and followed Owen's River Valley to its southern extremity. Desert Springs was the most southern point reached on the march to the rendezvous camp at Cottonwood Springs, Nevada; thence the line of travel was nearly due east, and most of the time followed the wagon-trail from Visalia, California, to the Ivanpah mines. This road crosses several ranges of mountains and is only available for wagons lightly loaded. In the vicinity of Camp Independence the ranges bordering the valley (that of Owen's River) are high, steep, and rugged, the Sierras on the west being in some localities quite heavily wooded. A large number of streams make down from these mountains and flow into Owen's River, and it is to these natural irrigation ditches that the valley owes its importance as an agricultural region. Many fine ranches are located all down the valley as far as near the lake, twenty-three miles from Independence, but below that point only the regular stations established at the springs along the road are met with.

The mountains grow lower as progress is made toward the south, in some places becoming mere rolling hills; this is particularly the case near the divide, between the Inyo and Coso Ranges, on the eastern side of the valley, where a broad expanse of country could be seen stretching off toward the Amargosa River and having all the appearance of being a perfect desert.

Desert Springs, one hundred and nineteen miles from Camp Independence, was reached August 15. The principal topographical features of interest noticed between Desert Springs and the Cottonwoods was the character of the valleys traversed. These valleys are simply inclosed basins, with a gradual slope to the south, terminating, in nearly every instance, in an alkali lake, generally dry. This is the case with Owen's River Valley, which, without doubt, formerly was drained into Needle Valley, where the waters, which now disappear by evaporation, and sinking into the earth at the two lakes below Independence, formerly lost themselves, leaving behind their saline constituents; and so on to the east, the presence of these flats or dry lakes indicate the localities of the sinks of waters which are drained from the high grounds of the valleys to the north and the mountains on either side.

The Amargosa River, about the course of which there has been considerable question, was carefully examined, and the result is as follows: nothing definite could be determined with regard to its source, but its general course was from the north to the south, and, making a complete change of direction about a point of rugged, volcanic mountains, near which Saratoga Spring is situated, it turns to the north again in the direction of Telescope Peak, on the western side of Death Valley; this would seem to indicate that Death Valley and the western branch of the valley of the Amargosa are the same. The results of my observations lead me to conclude that such is the case.

The general direction of the river, after turning to the north, can be followed for a long distance, running off into a deep desert valley; the mountains bordering it rise up, rugged and steep, with no foot-hills of any importance.

The country drained by the tributaries of the Amargosa extends east and west from Clarke Mountain, in the Ivanpah mining district, to Leach's Point, and the only indication of the existence of a river in this region is the bed, or wash, which marks its course. The character of the soil is such that the water sinks throughout the whole course of the stream, while the amount that disappears by evaporation, in consequence of the extreme heat that prevails throughout the year, is immense.

While at Saratoga Spring the thermometer indicated, between 4 and 5 p. m., a temperature of 112° F. in the shade, and at 9 p. m. the difference between the dry and wet bulb was 30°.

Nothing can exceed the utter desolation of this portion of California; the only vegetation that could be seen was an extremely scanty growth of greasewood, and even this disappears near the bottom of the valley, while for miles the river's banks are marked by a heavy deposition of various salts.

The soil on the higher ground is sandy and barren, and lower down is of a dark, reddish-brown color, and, at the time we passed, of about the consistency of stiff mortar, and yet there was no water on the surface; one ordinary rain would have rendered the course taken impracticable, and have necessitated a long detour to the south through the heavy sand.

At Saratoga Springs the water is warm and very alkaline. A scanty growth of grass about the spring afforded some relief to the eye, after the dull monotony of the surrounding desert, but not to the poor animals, who appear to derive but little benefit from it, and were growing visibly weaker each day. The water of the next spring to the east contains a large amount of salt in addition to the other ordinary alkaline ingredients, peculiar to the waters of this region. Only a very few of the animals would drink at this point, and they appeared to suffer considerably from so doing.

Ivanpah was reached on the 27th of August. No examination was made of the mines, you having expressed an intention of doing so yourself. So far as I could determine, however, the principal veins were quite narrow, and the ore in some cases very rich in silver.

Cottonwood Springs were reached August 30, without accident; from this point to Truxton Springs main party No. 1 was placed under my command with Lieutenant Lyle in executive charge. The following extract from Special Field Orders No. 20, dated September 2, 1871, will explain the character of my duties:

* * * * The interval from the departure of the river party from this camp, about September 7 to the 5th of October, will be occupied in examination by the main expedition, in Southeastern Nevada, Southwestern Utah, and to the point of crossing of the Colorado, the arrangements being somewhat as follows:

A small topographical party, in charge of F. R. Simonton, will proceed via Las Vegas Ranch to Mormon Wells, or Sheep Mountain Springs, north and east from Gass Peak, on Vegas Range; thence via head-waters of the Muddy, to join one of the main parties at the crossing of the old Salt Lake road. Another topographical party will be detached at Saint Joseph, to go via Saint Thomas, Salt Mountain, and across the Virgin Range. North and east to Saint George the main line of the expedition will continue along the old Salt Lake road as far as Saint George. From the old California crossing still another party will be detached to proced, via Mormon Cañon, Clover Valley, Shoal Creek, Mountain Meadows, &c., to Saint George. These will be known respectively as side parties 1, 2, and 3; the selection of persons to fill these parties will be made at once. A small topographical party will ascend Charleston Peak and return to this camp.

After reaching Saint George, the examinations should be along the area about the southeast corner of the reconnaissance map of 1869, and must be selected after reaching the above-named point. Probably routes may be selected along either side of the Buckskin Range of mountains, which at this locality is supposed to be a continuation of Wahsatch.

If possible, the best camp nearest the river, on a line sensibly joining Saint George and the point of crossing, should at once be selected for the rendezvous of the expedition. From this camp, Lieutenant Lyle, in charge of a small party of observation, will go out to select a favorable point at which to cross the river, which will take place upon the boats of the river party, this point being selected prior to the 5th proximo, with a view to a good camp, if possible, as well as a favorable outlet toward the south. Upon the arrival of the boat party at this point, immediate information will be sent to the land parties, who will at once make a hurried march for the river, where they will be crossed, and continue on at once to Peacock Springs. A small party of observation will remain at this point, and the boat party will continue the ascent of the river, reaching the cañon at the mouth of the Diamond River, if possible, to which point a party of relief and observation will be sent from Peacock Springs to take the party to camp. The time necessary for this party to wait at the mouth of the Diamond River cannot be stated until at the crossing of the river.

In case the boat party cannot reach the above-mentioned point they will fall back upon the small party of observation at the crossing, which, in consequence, must be re-enforced by riding and pack animals from Peacock Springs, after the main expedition shall have reached this point.

Lieutenant Lockwood is hereby placed in command of all the land parties, and Lieutenant Lyle in executive charge of main party No. 1, while both parties are together, and in entire and absolute charge of this party when it shall be separate.

GEO. M. WHEELER,
First Lieutenant, Corps of Engineers, Commanding Expedition.

Side parties were sent to Charleston Peak and Mormon Well. The march was resumed on the 15th of September, and on the 20th the Muddy River was reached, the march across the Vegas desert, forty-six miles long, having been made without accident. From here a side party was sent off via Clover Valley and Shoal Creek, to rejoin the expedition at Saint George. The wagon was sent across the desert to the same place via the old Salt Lake road, and the main parties followed up the Virgin River, reaching Saint George the 26th of September.

The country in the neighborhood of the Muddy River having been examined in 1869, and a report with regard to it made by yourself, I shall confine myself, concerning this locality, to speak simply of the changes that have taken place since then.

In 1869 the two settlements of Saint Joe and Saint Thomas were thriving towns, as Mormon industry is understood, while West Point, only just settled, bade fair, in time, to equal them in agricultural benefits and population. These settlements are now all deserted by their former inhabitants, they having left owing to the establishment of the fact that the places mentioned were in

9

the State of Nevada. I was informed that the people who formerly lived here are now settled some where in Arizona, about two hundred miles to the east of Saint George. The improvements at Saint Joe and at Saint Thomas have been sold to (so called) Gentiles, and will in time constitute valuable properties as the mineral resources of the adjacent country are opened up and markets for the products thus furnished. West Point has been left to the Indians, who show their appreciation of this act of compulsory generosity on the part of the Mormons by increased impudence (were that possible) to people passing near them.

This valley is one that, especially in the upper part, is capable of grazing a large amount of stock; all the cañons and washes leading down to the river are, as a general thing, heavily grassed, while the only water in the country around being that in the river, herding would be a simple matter.

The Virgin Mountains limit the valley of the river of that name to the east, and extend in an almost unbroken chain to within fifteen miles of Saint George, where the river breaks through them; in some parts these mountains are heavily wooded. To the west of the river a high mesa extends to the irregular, broken mountains lying east of the Mormon range. This mesa is cut up here and there by washes which carry the surface-waters to the Virgin River; formerly it was the scene of much suffering on the part of emigrants *en route* to Southern California, as the only water ever found is that which has collected in tanks and these dry up during the summer. Two roads cross it; one direct from Saint George, striking the Muddy near the old California crossing, and one which follows the river down to the Virgin Hill, and thence over to Saint Joe. This hill is practically impassable since the Mormons have abandoned the Muddy settlements, on account of the rain having washed off all the earth, leaving only the bare strata of rocks, which terminate in an abrupt staircase formation, extremely difficult even for loose animals.

Lieutenant Lyle was sent from Saint Thomas eastward over the Virgin Range of mountains, to find a suitable place for a temporary camp near the river, where the main parties might rendezvous until your arrival up the river at the point of crossing. A point near Pah-Koon Springs was selected by him as answering the above requirement.

The camp at Saint George was broken on the morning of October 1, and leaving Lieutenant Lyle in charge, I pushed forward to the river with a small party to select a point at which the crossing should be made. The route taken was down the Grand Wash, or near it; the Mormons had broken a sort of wagon-trail at some time in the past down this wash or cañon, and this was followed so far as practicable. I had expected, from previous information, to find a high range of mountains designated as the Buckskin Range, lying to the east of the Virgin Mountains, and limiting the area drained by the Grand Wash in that direction; instead, however, only an elevated mesa was seen, which near the river assumed a steep and rugged character, occasioned by the constant wash, in past ages, of waters seeking a lower level in the bed of the Colorado. For twenty miles north of the river the western edge of this mesa is nearly vertical, and curiously marked with bands of different colors, showing the stratification. To the north this mesa joins a vast wooded plateau, which extends to what is called Hurricane Valley, on the Virgin River, forty miles above Saint George.

Your opportune arrival with your boats the morning after I reached the river, rendered it unnecessary for the train to remain any length of time at Pah-Koon Springs, and on the morning of October 6th everything was across the river and ready to proceed to Truxton Springs. The freight was ferried over on the evening of the 5th, requiring only four hours, and the animals swam the stream the next morning. One horse had a leg broken among the rocks; otherwise there was no accident of any kind. Truxton Springs were reached on the evening of October 10th, where the detachment of C troop, Third Cavalry, detailed as escort, had already arrived.

The first march out from the river was to Tin-na-kah Springs, near the foot of what is known as the Colorado Plateau. The trail to it leads up a broad wash, the formation continuing for some distance the same as on the river. The walls of the cañon are nearly vertical for a long distance, and are marked by the different strata in various colors; gradually, however, the country assumes an alluvial character, the sandy washes and the sterile gravel mesas giving place to grassy plateaus and occasional mesquit, and then little clumps of cedars attest the increased fertility of the soil.

Several rugged peaks and ridges are found near Tin-na-kah, and all are more or less volcanic in their formation and character. Ten miles from the springs the trail strikes up on to the main plateau. From here a fine view of the country north of the Colorado could be obtained. The North Side Mountain, a high conical peak, could be seen standing out alone on the vast mesa beyond the Grand Cañon; but no range that occupied the locality assigned to the Buckskin Mountains could be observed. I am inclined to believe that the name has been erroneously given to the edge of the plateau, which extends on to the north from the mouth of the Grand Cañon. This vast plateau extends over the whole of Northern Arizona, from near Hualapais Valley to the east. Throughout its whole extent, at least that portion which I passed over, the rolling hills are, as a general thing, covered with grass. The trail, after attaining the summit of the plateau, follows along its western edge, bordering Hualapais Valley until within eight miles of Truxton Springs, at which point it descends a steep hill, and gaining a sandy wash lower down, follows it out to near its mouth, where the springs are situated. Upon my arrival here I found the rations that were to have been there had not arrived. The two wagons that had been sent along to furnish transportation for the escort from Hualapais were immediately despatched to Camp Mohave for supplies, and Lieutenant Lyle, with a small escort, went on to Hualapais to bring the mail and obtain such articles as were most needed.

Dr. Hoffman was sent to the mouth of the Diamond Creek, but by some mistake did not take the right trail, and went on to Young's Spring. On the 18th Mr. Loring came in, bringing a dispatch from you, and on the following morning I took charge of a small party of relief to meet you at the mouth of the Diamond Creek. The trail to that point leads up a box cañon from Truxton, and passing over a rolling divide, gains a side cañon, which joins the Diamond Creek about two miles from its mouth. Peach Spring is situated about midway. The cañon leading into Diamond Creek is of the same general character as all the Colorado cañons, having steep, rugged walls, in some places nearly vertical, and unbroken for a height of one thousand feet or more. In the vicinity of Peach Spring the slopes are wooded with cedar, and the whole country traversed covered with grass, except in the gravelly beds of the washes. On the 21st the party started back, reaching Truxton on the evening of the 22d.

FROM TRUXTON SPRINGS TO PRESCOTT.

On the 24th my party started for Prescott, moving out nearly due east, following for three days the guide-stakes established by the railroad surveying party, which had preceded me only a short time at Truxton. The country was found to be a series of terraced plateaus, each one to the east growing in height, and being gained by following up an easy grade through cañons leading to their summits; these different table-lands have all the appearance of being regular mountain ranges when seen from the west; the slopes in many cases are covered with timber. No water was found after leaving Young's Spring until the volcanic country, nearly northwest from Mount Floyd, was reached. Here the plateau is cut up by box cañons in the volcanic rock, and in many of them large reservoirs have been formed where the water collects during the rainy season and generally remains throughout the year, the temperature not being sufficiently great to evaporate the whole.

Mount Floyd is an irregular mountain north of the Juniper Range, and is surrounded on all sides by strong evidences of volcanic agency. The whole country is strewn with eruptive matter, and cut up by narrow box cañons, which are impassable except at certain points; the general direction of all these old water-beds was to the south, about the southern point of Bill Williams' Mountain, emptying into the Verde. The *Red butte*, mentioned by Ives, could be seen standing out by itself to the north, and beyond it what appeared to be an elevated table-land, considerably higher than the one upon which we then were.

The trail led about to the north of Bill Williams' Mountain, until the San Francisco Mountains and Sunset Crossing road to Albuquerque, New Mexico, was reached; this was then followed out through Chino Valley to Prescott. Mr. Gilbert, chief geologist, ascended the mountain (Bill Williams') with a small party. Barometrical observations to obtain its height were taken, and a careful examination of the character of the formation made by that gentleman, the results of which will appear in his report. The foot-hills all about, and the mountain itself, are covered with a heavy growth of pine, and occasional oak thickets are found.

The road, after leaving the mountain, gains the valley beyond by a series of very heavy grades, crosses Hell and Rattlesnake Cañons, of volcanic origin, and breaking through a rough, rugged range of hills, gains Chino Valley; from this point to Prescott there is a fine track. The Juniper Mountains, lying to the southwest of Bill Williams, are low, rolling hills, and densely wooded. In the report of Lieutenant Ives this country is called the Black Forest. To the east of Chino Valley are the Black Hills, very rugged, with extremely steep slopes; these hills constitute one of the many strongholds of the Apache-Mohave Indians. The country to the north is cut up with box cañons which extend to the Verde beyond, and the approaches on all sides are so difficult that in nearly all cases pursuit of the Indians in this vicinity is attended with very meager results.

Prescott was reached on the night of October 31, where I found Dr. Cochrane had already arrived with main party No. 1.

PRESCOTT TO CAMP APACHE.

Leaving Prescott on the 10th of November, main party No. 2 took the road leading out through Agua Fria Valley, and crossing the Black Hills descended into the valley of the Verde River. The mountains limiting this valley are quite high, and very rugged. The eastern range may be considered as the edge of the vast elevated plateau already spoken of, and the summit once gained, the scene presented is nearly the same as that farther to the west. The prevalence of loose volcanic matter, scattered over the country, constituting what are termed Malpais Plains, renders the traversing of this section a very difficult matter during the seasons of rain; the same irregular formation of mesa ridges is observed here as to the west of Bill Williams' Mountain.

Sunset Crossing was reached on the 17th of November; just before reaching this point, and while on the summit of a slight rise in the mesa, the view in every direction showed only the vast rolling table-land, with occasional ridges, except toward San Francisco Mountain to the north, which appeared to rise up abruptly from the plain.

The Colorado Chiquito was followed as far as Leroux Fork, where the road to Camp Apache leaves the Santa Fé road, and, turning to the south, breaks through the Mogollon Mountains, reaching the valley of the Salt River and its tributaries. These mountains constitute the watershed between the Little Colorado and Salt Rivers, and may be described, generally, as a low, rolling range, covered with loose volcanic matter, and heavily wooded with pine. The appearance of this range changes entirely when viewed from the south, as the elevation of the plateau to the north is so great that the descent from it to the lower country of the Salt River and tributaries, by the abrupt slopes peculiar to the southern limit of the Colorado Plateau, gives all the features that are observed in ordinary mountain ranges, so that, while viewed from near the Little Colorado, the Mogollon Mountains are merely heavily wooded, low, rolling hills; from the south they appear to break out as a veritable range of high mountains. The White Mountains could be seen in the distance, but no near approach was made to them.

At Camp Apache the Colorado plateau proper was left by my party, and thence to the Gila the trail leads over the Natanes mesa, and the Apache and Pinal ranges of mountains. The country to the southwest of the camp is rough, and broken by deep cañons, which have their outlets in the Salt, or Prieto, River; the latter is the name given to the Salt River above the point where its course lies through the salt-beds that completely change its character. At the point where the trail crosses it, the river breaks through a deep cañon, the southern bank being 1,950 feet above the water; reaching the summit, a broad, rolling plateau is seen, which is a continuation of the Natanes Mountains. To the west, the irregular line of the opposite wall of an extensive box cañon was readily discerned, where the river's course is extremely tortuous. The walls appeared to be red sandstone; the country beyond, to the west, was very much broken and cut up by vast cañons, which headed off in the direction of the Sierra Ancha, and particularly near Sombrero Butte. The confusion created by nature was truly wonderful.

The Natanes mesa is a broad rolling plateau, cut up by cañons leading into the Salt River; these are in most places practically impassable and have to be headed. Descending, the trail leads down into the valley of the west fork of the San Carlos River, which heads within a few miles of the Salt River and empties into the Gila. Crossing this, a steep, rugged range, known as the Apache Mountains, was next crossed, and again we were in the country drained by the tributaries of the Salt River.

The Apache Mountains form a short range, which extends from the mouth of Pinal Creek about twenty miles to the east, slightly turning to the north. The slopes on both sides are extremely steep, and the foot-hills terminate in long, gently sloping ridges, formed by the deep washes which run toward the branches of the San Carlos on the north and Pinal Creek on the south.

In June last, while making a reconnaissance in this country with Captain Evan Miles, Twenty-first Infantry, the region where the mountains head, on Salt River, was visited; the range was found to continue unbroken to within a few miles of the river, where a remarkably steep slope leads down to a broad, sandy wash, running off to the west, and reaching the river nearly due south of Sombrero Butte. Pinal Creek was followed up to where it heads in the mountains of that name, which were crossed by an extremely difficult trail leading across Papoose Cañon on Pinto Creek. The trail then leads through a rough, broken country, covered with granite rocks and bowlders, to Camp Pinal, (abandoned,) which is situated on the head-waters of Mineral Creek, a tributary of the Gila. Onward from this point, the evidences of volcanic agency were everywhere encountered. The cañons of Mineral Creek are 200 or 300 feet deep, and form almost perfect types, in places, of what are known as "box cañons;" their walls are nearly vertical, and the rock in which they are formed is generally basalt, occurring in huge columns, while the surrounding country is strewn with lava and immense bowlders. Everywhere the eye, at first glance, sees only broken, rocky ridges and deep gulches, which appear impassable by the ordinary means of transportation. After leaving the Pinal Mountains, which have a regularity of form quite remarkable, the ranges crossed were much broken, being cut up in all directions, with no regular trend. This character extends through to the Mazatzal Range, and in fact nearly to the Verde River.

A curious point, called Weaver's Needle, is seen off to the west, and appears in the distance to be simply a huge rock, as its slopes are too steep for earth or even loose *débris*.

Superstition Mountain, about twenty miles west, is remarkable from the peculiar marking of the stratification by broad bands of various colors, which extend for miles and maintain an almost perfect parallelism. The face of this mountain is formed in regular steps or terraces, often several hundred feet in height.

The valley of the Gila is through a gravelly mesa, and varies in width from a few hundred yards to several miles. I have seen sections through this mesa cut by the water up near the mountains, and for thirty feet the sand, gravel, and rocks were arranged in regular order, the gravel and rocks being cemented together, so that the walls were nearly vertical.

From Florence, where I first struck the Gila, the road to Tucson, via the Picacho, was taken. The so-called Picacho Pass is a broad opening between two separate ranges of volcanic mountains, having no relation to each other, except the accidental circumstance of having their axes in nearly the same line. The pass, without doubt, is merely an extension of the mesa. The mountains rise abruptly from the plain, having no foot-hills, and no signs are visible of anything like a connection between them having ever existed. The well at the station, eight miles from the Picacho, is nearly 200 feet deep, and the proprietor informed me that the water-vein very much resembled an underground river of considerable size. As this is near the old line marked down as the underground course of the Santa Cruz, it is quite likely that the well, by good fortune, has struck it.

From this point the road passes over a vast plain, having small alkali flats scattered along it, until reaching the Santa Cruz River, which it crosses and follows to Tucson. The hills and mountains in the vicinity have a rugged, volcanic aspect, and, as a general thing, rise abruptly from the plain, with no foot-hills of any importance.

AGRICULTURAL LANDS.

The amount of agricultural land in Owen's River Valley is limited at present by the facilities for irrigation. In consequence of the river's course being in soft alkali soil through the middle and lowest part of the valley, its bed has sunk so far below the surface of the ground that its waters are not available for irrigation, except near its source. The small streams that rise high in the mountains, and flow down and across the valley, are thoroughly utilized, and it is to them that this region owes its importance, agriculturally speaking. Below the lake the valley is a barren desert, and, with but one or two exceptions, there is no land available for cultivation.

Passing east, the same general character obtains until the Cottonwood Springs are reached, where the Indians cultivate a few acres, raising pumpkins, melons, and corn. No white man has deemed this place as affording sufficient prospects of success to justify even his settling there for any time. About the Vegas Springs two ranches have been located recently, with good success to the settlers. Considerably more might be taken up were the supply of water more extensive. In addition to what was under cultivation at the Vegas ranch in 1869, about 80 acres may be mentioned as having been planted during the last year, but the proprietors state that the supply of water would be insufficient for any more. Peach-trees have been started here and are stated to produce finely.

The amount of land available on the Muddy and Virgin Rivers has already been estimated by yourself, and it is probable that a considerable deduction for the extent actually under cultivation at present should be made, since the Mormons, who were compelled to utilize every foot of ground that could be irrigated to support their surplus population, have abandoned the country.

In the vicinity of Saint George there are about 2,000 acres under cultivation, all that can be irrigated, in fact. A project was started, some years ago, to change the course of the Virgin River, and by carrying it, with a slight fall, higher up toward the table-lands, open up a vast extent of country which, except in certain seasons, is only useful on account of the scanty pasturage it affords. This scheme was baulked, after a vast expense had been incurred, by difficulties encountered in tunneling through a small range of mountains. The grand ditch was to start thirty or forty miles above Saint George, and, if successful, would have increased by ten-fold the amount of country now under cultivation.

There are quite a number of small, scattering towns near Saint George, but I am unable to state aught with regard to their facilities for agriculture; only those in the immediate vicinity are included in the above estimate.

From Saint George to Chino Valley, north of Prescott, only a few Indian farms were seen; those may consist of from twenty to two hundred hills of corn, a few pumpkin-vines, melons, and squashes; they do not, as a general thing, average much more, and what they do produce is, for the most part, eaten before reaching maturity.

Chino Valley has about 3,000 or 4,000 acres extending to near Prescott, and the principal product is corn; potatoes and onions are raised to some extent.

The next arable land met with was in the Agua Fria Valley, the principal ranch being that of Mr. Bowers. I should judge that from 1,500 to 2,000 acres are here cultivated. Corn is mainly the staple product.

The Gila bottom can be cultivated throughout when the supply of water obtainable from the river is sufficiently great. A broad strip on each side of the river has been taken up by farmers, and from three miles above Florence to Maricopa Wells the country is being utilized; the principal product now is barley, in consequence of the large amount required at the various military posts throughout the country. At the Pima villages (Indian reservation) a considerable quantity of wheat is annually produced. At Gila Bend a large irrigation ditch, fifteen miles in length, is being taken out, and, when completed, will open up a large tract of valuable land. At Phœnix, on the Salt River, about 10,000 acres are under cultivation, and here companies have been formed to construct proper ditches, &c. The lands along the rivers produce very large crops of barley; and the markets are generally good.

All, or nearly all, this region was formerly cultivated by a race which has entirely disappeared from the country. This is shown by the ruins of vast acequias located, in some instances, where farmers of the present day have never thought of going. At Phœnix, where the irrigation ditches are on a very extensive scale for modern enterprise, I have seen the ruins of a vast canal three or four miles outside of any that have yet been attempted in this vicinity. A project is on foot, however, to open up the old acequia, and when this is done a large extent of country will be opened up, giving ample security for success to many more settlers.

Growths of mesquit have sprung up since the former inhabitants left this country, in some places forming impenetrable barriers for miles along the rivers; these having been cleared away, the ground, in all cases, is found prepared for irrigation, perfectly smooth, with the slopes properly arranged.

With regard to the available land about Tucson I can state nothing, as my stay there was only for a few hours, and my opportunities for obtaining information on that subject consequently limited.

GRAZING-LANDS.

The grass found in Owen's River Valley is either that which grows in the bottom-lands or the scattered growth found in the foot-hills and mountains. The grass on bottom-lands that have been cultivated is of very fair quality, but generally is of an alkaline character, on account of the alkali matter in the soil. The bunch-grass in the mountains is admirably adapted to animals getting but little or no grain.

On the route traveled by myself through Southern California but little grazing was met with until near Ivanpah and Cottonwood Springs. Here there are vast tracts covered with sand and bunch-grass; along the Muddy, particularly near West Point, there is a fine opportunity for an enterprising stock-raiser.

About Saint George there is but little grass, but at the head of the Grand Wash ample range for a large number of animals exists.

The Colorado plateau, particularly that portion over which my route extended, is covered with a fine growth of nutritious grasses, and in time, when the Indians are sufficiently subdued to permit of it, this whole country will afford as fine facilities for raising stock as any country I have ever visited on the Pacific slope. The supply of water is sufficient for vast herds, and not being scattered as in some localities, the stock could be easily managed.

The whole country along my route of travel, from Prescott to Camp Pinal, was through grassy uplands of vast extent. What grass is found upon the mesas bordering the Gila bottom is very excellent in quality and stock thrive well upon it. The great difficulty is that the stock is rarely driven from the lowlands in consequence of the danger apprehended from the sudden raids of Indians who watch the herds from the mountains and drive them off with little or no difficulty. Pursuit generally avails little, and the only satisfaction the owners usually have is that caused by finding the remains of an extensive feast that has been served up at their expense.

WOOD-LANDS.

The valleys of Southern California and Nevada sustain only a scanty growth of greasewood, and in some localities sage-brush. Generally, however, in the Sierras and the more elevated mountains white-pine and scrub-cedar are found. This obtains in the Clarke Mountains at Ivanpah, and in the Spring Mountains at Potosi, and to the north.

In the mountains about Saint George considerable pine is found, and at the head of the Grand Wash a dense growth of cedar.

The Colorado plateau is densely wooded in some localities. Near the western limit thickets of scrub-cedar and some pine are found. The Black Forest, mentioned by Lieutenant Ives, is a dense growth of juniper.

Near Bill Williams' Mountain the timber is principally pine with a few scrub-oaks. Along the road from Camp Verde to Camp Apache, especially near the edge of the Colorado plateau, heavy growths of pine and juniper are met with.

Camp Apache is in a heavily wooded district. The Mogollon Mountains and the country near the east and west forks of White Mountain River are covered with pine and juniper. The Natanes mesa is also well wooded, and the Pinal Mountains, farther south; the creek of that name is bordered with cottonwoods, and near its source a few oaks are found, and generally the mountain country north of the site of Camp Pinal is more or less heavily wooded with pine and juniper.

In the country to the south and along the Gila, cottonwoods are found near the river, while mesquit and palo verde grow farther back, on the edge of the mesa; beyond this only stray mesquit and greasewood are noticed, and an occasional palo verde.

MINERAL LANDS AND MINES.

The principal mines along the route were those in the Slate Range district and the Johnson district, Ivanpah, the mines on Lynx Creek, near Prescott, and the mines in the Black Hills, near Camp Verde.

The Slate Range mines are so named from the mountains in which they are situated; they have been deserted for several years in consequence of the failure of the company working them.

The principal and best yielding are the black ores, known as stromeyerite and stedefeldtite; the ledges are narrow and between slate walls. One tunnel had been run 500 feet, but failed to reach the ledge at that distance. Machinery for milling gold-ore, found near, have been erected, but the results obtained were not remunerative, and, the funds of the company being soon exhausted, the whole district was abandoned. Some of the former owners now state that if the amount expended in working low-grade gold-rock had been applied properly to the development of the silver leads the result would have been different. With regard to this I cannot give an opinion, as the imperfect knowledge acquired by me of the locality of these mines was insufficient to enable me to find them.

The Johnson district is near Desert Springs, and all the leads discovered are composed of lead and copper. Nothing has been done toward developing the district; no assays have been made, and the mines are not valued very highly. Several specimens were obtained and have been added to your collection.

The Ivanpah mines having been visited and examined by yourself, no report from me is necessary.

The mines near Prescott, on Lynx Creek, are worked only for free gold. But little has been done here except to prospect in a rude manner. The old Mexican arrastra is used, and with it the ore yields from $20 to $45 per ton. Some of the shafts are down 25 feet and show well-defined walls nearly vertical.

The vein-matter is very much disintegrated, most of it crumbling easily in the hand with a slight pressure. Assays have been made several times by assayers at Prescott, but their results were so unsatisfactory that they were not given. The whole bed of the creek has been dug over, and in some places quite rich deposits of placer gold have been found. The prevailing opinion is that the placer diggings have all been worked over once, probably by the race of beings the record of whose existence consists now only in the curious ruins occasionally found and the fragments of pottery scattered over the country.

At present but very little is being done here; a few prospectors who are able to obtain sufficient water are taking out a little gold, but only enough to purchase supplies with which to live. The Indians have killed several miners, and small parties are consequently deterred from locating here. Nearly all the creeks and ravines near Lynx Creek show gold in small quantities, not enough, however, to cause any extensive operations to be inaugurated; and the few mills that have been started are now deserted and have been for some time. With improved methods of working these deposits they may in time be made to pay, but the supply of water is limited, and this will always prove a great drawback to anything like extensive operations.

NATURAL HISTORY.

Dr. Hoffman accompanied my party as naturalist from the crossing of the river to the termination of the field-work at Tucson. Throughout the season Mr. Bischoff was collector in natural history. The specimens obtained by him are very extensive, comprising many that are new.

GEOLOGY.

From Camp Independence to Cottonwoods, and from Truxton Springs to Prescott, Mr. G. K. Gilbert, chief geologist, accompanied my party as geologist. Mr. Marvine had charge of this department from Prescott to Tucson. The reports of these gentlemen will, I understand, be given you.

METEOROLOGY.

At all rendezvous camps hourly observations were taken, as follows: Barometric readings, using cistern and aneroid barometers; wet and dry bulb thermometric readings were also taken;

10

the direction of the wind was also observed, and its force as determined with an anemometer. The general record also included the character and amount of clouds, time of beginning and ending of rain and snow storms, and the amount of fall. Also such phenomena as would be included under the general head of meteorological data.

At ordinary camps, observations were taken at 7 a. m., 2 p. m., and 9 p. m., or where the time of going into or breaking camp was such as to render this impossible, observations were taken upon arriving and upon leaving, and the hours noted. Observations were taken while on the march at the topographical stations with an aneroid, carefully compared with a cistern barometer.

MEANS OF COMMUNICATION, ROUTES FOR ROADS, ETC.

The road from Independence to Desert Wells is the regular stage-route from Los Angeles to Owen's River Valley. The one from Visalia to Ivanpah is one over which but very little travel has ever passed.

Burnt Rock Cañon will have to be very much improved by lessening the grade, which can only be accomplished by blasting out the solid rock, before heavily-loaded wagons can attempt this route with any prospect of being able to get through.

The bottom of the Amargosa is impassable except after the hot weather has dried up the soft alkali mud; this limits the availability of this route to a very few months in the year. At other times the trail through the sand-hills to the south would be the only course that could be taken. From this point to Ivanpah, the heavy sand in places will always be a great drawback, but need not be considered as closing the route. Nearly every road in Southern California and Nevada may be described as very good or very bad; the former obtains when traversing the gravel mesas, and the latter when following up the sandy washes or in crossing, in wet weather, the numerous alkali flats in this region. The road from the Cottonwoods to Saint George is no exception to this rule, and the vast amount of freight that has been transported over the old Salt Lake road, from Los Angeles to interior Utah, is sufficient proof of the availability of this route.

To establish a road from Saint George south to the Ute crossing for heavy wagons would require considerable labor; first, in getting over the mountains just south of the Virgin where the grades are remarkably steep and rocky; and again to get out of the Grand Wash and into the smaller one which reaches the river two miles below the Ute crossing. The road, to be available, would have to leave the Grand Wash, as at its mouth the landing on the opposite side of the river is not practicable.

From the river to Truxton Springs there would be but little difficulty encountered, and that only in ascending the plateau beyond Tin-na-kah Springs, and in descending the mountains into the wash leading into Truxton. From here a regular road leads down to the south, striking the Mohave and Prescott road near the Cottonwoods, five miles west of old Camp Willow Grove.

The route from Verde to Camp Apache is traveled at all times except when blocked by the snow in winter.

During the rainy season the Malpais region from Beaver Creek over the mountains is very heavy, and only lightly-loaded teams can get through without encountering considerable difficulty.

There has been no feasible route found from Camp Apache to Tucson via Camp Pinal, except for pack-trains.

INDIANS.

After leaving Owen's River Valley no Indians were seen until Ivanpah was reached; here there are quite a number, who, for the most part, are employed by the miners to carry water to the mines, This idea of labor is not applicable to the men, as they as a general thing are perfectly contented to enjoy the fruits of the labors of their squaws; some few, however, who have been for a long time with the whites, work at times, but it is safe to state only when compelled by hunger. They belong to the tribe of Pi-Utes, or Pah-Utes, as do also the Indians at Cottonwood Springs, Vegas, along the Muddy, and at Saint George. At present those at Ivanpah are perfectly harmless, but only from realizing the superiority of the whites over them. Two years ago, when the mining camp was occupied by only a few men, the majority having gone to Visalia and Los Angeles for provisions, they entered the town and compelled the few people left behind to cook for them what little in the way of provisions was left. Fortunately the wagons arrived while this was going on, and the Indians were driven off; they returned in a few days, however, and asked for food. At the time I passed through I should judge there were nearly one hundred in all encamped about Ivanpah.

At Cottonwood Springs and at Las Vegas there are quite a large number, who move backward and forward between the two places, according to their fancy. They have small farms or gardens, and besides the corn, pumpkins, melons, &c., raised by themselves, obtain scanty supplies from the Vegas ranches for what little work they do. Occasionally they commit some depredation, but the prompt and severe punishment they always receive from the whites, when found out, as a general thing keeps them quiet. I should estimate that these met with at Cottonwood Springs and Las Vegas would number about two hundred. They lead a life of perfect indolence, with a few exceptions, and seem to prefer their present precarious mode of living to one the security of which must depend upon their own exertions and labors.

But little change has taken place among the Indians along the Muddy, except that, not feeling the restraint formerly put upon them by the presence of the Mormons, they are now extremely impudent and bold. They are great beggars, and on several occasions strongly hinted their intentions of taking what they wanted if their demands were not complied with; this, however, was never attempted, and I think it only requires the presence of five or six determined men to keep them at a respectful distance. They are well supplied, and the facilities afforded them for raising grain are not equaled by those of any other band in this portion of Nevada.

The Indians at Saint George are quiet and peaceable, many of them working regularly for the Mormons. Long and continued association with the whites has accomplished this perfect change in their character. It was observed, however, that the converts had generally been raised from infancy away from immediate contact with their own people. Many of the Indians referred to have horses and ponies, and all are usually well clothed.

At Tin-na-kah Spring a deserted rancheria with a small garden was seen, but no Indians were met until Cañon Springs were reached; these belonged to the Hualapais tribe, and seemed very much frightened at seeing us. They had all left their rancherias when we came up, and were out in the hills; they came in after awhile and began begging. Between Tin-na-kah and the crossing of New River, several broad, well-beaten trails were seen, all seeming to converge toward some point on New River, near the Colorado. I afterward learned that this locality was formerly a great hiding-place for the Hualapais, when hard pushed during the war which resulted in their being partially brought to terms, so much so, in fact, that many of them now submit to receiving from the Government, as gifts, that which they formerly insisted upon taking in their own way.

The Hualapais at Truxton Springs are not so wild as those seen at Cañon Springs. They nearly all are fed at Beale Springs by the Government, and are consequently more accustomed to the sight of white men. I can give no estimate of their number, as they were coming and going all the time we were there.

To the east, in the vicinity of Diamond Creek, a small band was met with, known as the Seviches. They are a finely developed race, bold and warlike, and regard the approach of the white man into their territory with jealous distrust. They always left their rancherias as we approached and hid themselves in the hills; they would afterward come suddenly into camp, and, although manifesting a seemingly great desire to shake hands with every one, would evince their doubts by always asking what we wanted, coupling with this question a rather peremptory request for tobacco. These Indians have gardens at Peach Spring and at the head of Diamond Creek. Their country is well supplied with game, and they all appeared capable of taking care of themselves. They did not allow the squaws to come in sight at all.

No Indians were seen again until reaching Camp Verde, although throughout Chino and Agua Fria Valley they frequently commit depredations. The ranchmen always take their rifles with them; and it is a common occurrence for herders to be picked off, or men shot, while at work in the fields. The Apache-Mohaves roam through this region, and their country extends east to the mountains beyond the Verde River. At the post of that name several hundred were being fed. Quite a large number were found at Beaver Creek, and although then *en route* to the post to get their five days' allowance, showed great insolence to a small advanced guard that preceded the party. I have since learned that these Indians have all left the reservation.

At Camp Apache nearly twelve hundred were being fed, and seemed peaceable and well contented. Last May, however, they drove off the herds, and for a long time remained away from the post. These Indians belong to the Coyotero, or White Mountain Apache tribe, and have committed many depredations in this country, and even as far south as the roads leading out from Tucson.

The next tribe to the south are the Pinal Apaches, who live in the country about the Pinal Mountains. None of them were seen; they are very wild and warlike, refusing to go upon reservations or have any communication whatever with white men. Their country is very rough, and scouting parties encounter great difficulties in hunting them.

The general character of the Apache Indians is too well understood to require any further mention from me than that my experience in their country leads me to conclude that their bloodthirsty nature has not been overdrawn. In time, perhaps, civilizing influences might render them less wild and barbarous than they now are; but this change I do not consider as likely to happen except in the case of those taken at an early age from their own people.

In conclusion, I would express my indebtedness to the different assistants who were with me for their co-operation and valuable aid in bringing the labors of the season to so successful a termination.

Respectfully submitted.

DANIEL W. LOCKWOOD,
First Lieutenant of Engineers.

Lieutenant GEO. M. WHEELER,
Corps of Engineers.

APPENDIX B.

Report of Second Lieutenant D. A. Lyle, Second United States Artillery.

UNITED STATES ENGINEER OFFICE,
EXPLORATIONS IN NEVADA AND ARIZONA,
Washington, D. C., March 5, 1872.

SIR: In compliance with your letter of instructions, dated February 15, 1872, I have the honor to submit the following preliminary report:

I assumed command of the escort, a detachment of twenty-five men from Troop I, Third United States Cavalry, and also of main party No. 2 of the expedition, by virtue of the following orders:

Special Field Orders }
    No. 10.—Extract.   }

UNITED STATES ENGINEER OFFICE,
EXPLORATIONS IN NEVADA AND ARIZONA,
Camp near Belmont, Nevada, June 23, 1871.

*   *   *   *   *   *   *   *   *

I. Second Lieutenant D. A. Lyle, Second United States Artillery, having reported in obedience to paragraph I, Special Orders No. 98, Headquarters Military Division of the Pacific, is hereby placed in command of the escort, and, until the arrival of First Lieutenant D. W. Lockwood, Corps of Engineers, in charge of party No. 2 of the exploration.

GEO. M. WHEELER,
First Lieutenant, United States Engineers, Commanding Expedition.

Special Field Orders }
    No. 16.   }

UNITED STATES ENGINEER OFFICE,
EXPLORATIONS IN NEVADA AND ARIZONA,
Rendezvous Camp near Belmont, Nevada, July 2, 1871.

Main party No. 2 of the exploration, under command of Second Lieutenant D. A. Lyle, Second United States Artillery, will proceed at daylight to-morrow (Monday) morning, *en route* to Camp Independence, California, on the trunk-line selected from this point to the rendezvous camp at the above-named station. He will be furnished with a copy of the letter of instructions from the Chief of Engineers of the 22d of March, 1871, and will, in all respects, adhere thereto, conducting his party in the same manner as if it were a separate expedition. Fifteen days will be allowed to reach Camp Independence, and *en route* special attention must be given to the examinations in the contiguous mining districts.

He will be called upon for a report of his trip.

By command of Lieutenant Wheeler.

D. A. LYLE,
Second Lieutenant, Second Artillery, Adjutant of the Expedition.

Accordingly, on the morning of the 3d of July, I left the rendezvous camp in Meadow Creek Cañon, north of Belmont, Nevada, and set out upon the march

FROM BELMONT, NEVADA, TO CAMP INDEPENDENCE, CALIFORNIA.

Following down Meadow Creek Cañon for several miles we struck the stage-road from Austin to Belmont; thence crossing the Toquima Range and Ralston Valley, in a southwesterly direction, we encamped at Cedar Springs (Baxter's Station) on west side of valley, having marched thirty and a quarter miles. Here we found plenty of wood and good water, but very little grass.

Ralston Valley is from eight to twelve miles wide, a sandy, gravelly, stony desert, with no vegetation except wild sage. At this point a wagon-road comes in from the southeast from Reveille.

The next day made a short march of eleven miles to Indian Springs, (San Antonio,) in Big Smoky Valley. Here we found plenty of water, slightly brackish, little grass, and no wood except sage-brush. The route to this point was upon a wagon-road, from Belmont to San Antonio and Fish Lake Valley. The road from Cedar Springs lies over a low range, through an excellent pass, bordered with plenty of nut-pine and cedar, but no grass or water. There are two quartz-mills at this point, both lying idle; some arable land, but natural facilities for irrigation are limited. If irrigated the soil would be productive. Jack rabbits and mountain quail the only game seen.

My orders being discretionary with regard to everything except time and general direction of line, I concluded to detach at this point a small topographical party, consisting of Acting Assistant Surgeon W. J. Hoffman, United States Army, in charge, one topographer, two civilian assistants, with a packer, guide, and soldier, to visit San Antonio mining district, and follow down the west side of the San Antonio Range, pushing their investigations to the east and southeast, and passing to the east of Lone Mountains to Montezuma; then crossing the mountains, after visiting the

Montezuma mines and entering Clayton Valley, this party was to join the main party at Silver Peak, while myself with the latter party crossed the Smoky Valley Desert to the west and southwest of Lone Mountains, via Desert Wells, where, instead of crossing the low summit of the Toyabe Range to the westward into Fish Lake Valley, as previously intended, we would move southeasterly into Clayton Valley to Silver Peak, in order to facilitate the junction of the detached side party, presuming that the topographical and physical results would be more fertile on this line than they could possibly be by crossing directly into Fish Lake Valley to the north of Red Mountains. This presumption was fully sustained by subsequent results.

On the 5th the main party crossed this desert, reaching Desert Wells at 5 p. m., having made thirty-two miles, very hot and dusty, both men and animals suffering severely from thirst, the result of drinking brackish water at Indian Springs. Here we found three springs filled with slimy mud, from which we could get no water. About half a mile to the northeast was a large hole containing a few gallons of water.

We concluded to bivouac here for a few hours to rest and feed the animals preparatory to making a night march to Silver Peak, twenty-five miles distant. By dint of considerable digging, at which we all took turns, we procured enough water to supply our wants and those of the animals partially, though it was very brackish and alkaline.

The country traversed this day was a sandy desert, covered with wild sage, and toward the lower end of the valley interspersed with hard, white alkali flats, destitute of vegetation. Jack rabbits, lizards, and beetles were the only specimens of animated nature seen. Owing to the cloudiness of the weather and the darkness it was not until 2 o'clock a. m. that we resumed our march to the southeast, and skirting for several miles an alkali lake, (dry,) some twelve miles long and from one to six miles wide, we passed up a rocky wash and crossed a low ridge or divide connecting Red Mountain Range with Lone Mountains. This ridge was composed of volcanic remains—lava flows, extinct volcanoes, volcanic ashes, scoria, and basalt; native sulphur and alum being also met with.

Entering Clayton Valley we passed a very perfect volcanic cone of recent date, but now extinct, and striking a salt marsh, twelve to fifteen miles long and from four to eight miles wide, we arrived at Silver Peak. Here is a cluster of saline springs, mostly warm, and of various degrees of saturation, one of which was constantly boiling; the waters were impregnated with salt, lime, borax, and sulphur. Another very remarkable spring was one out in the salt marsh about half a mile, which was nearly fresh, and the water quite cold. The white surface of this marsh was broken by two or three rocky *buttes*, upon which trilobites and other fossils were found; toward the lower part of the valley were shifting sand-hills.

Here we remained till the 8th of July, recuperating ourselves and animals, awaiting the arrival of Dr. Hoffman and party. This interval was devoted to investigations of a geographical, geological, and mineralogical nature. Astronomical and meteorological observations were also made. I visited the mines in the Silver Peak and Red Mountain mining districts, which are owned by the Silver Peak and Red Mountain Gold and Silver Mining Company, who have a 30-stamp gold-mill at this point. For the details regarding these mines I would respectfully invite your attention to my report on "Mines and mining districts," appended and marked A.

Clayton Valley is a complete interior basin, being surrounded on all sides by mountains. It is about eighteen or twenty miles long, and from eight to fifteen miles wide, the longer axis being nearly north and south. There is plenty of grass in the vicinity of the springs, but poor in quality, and no wood nearer than the summit of the main ridge, about ten miles from the mill.

Upon taking a cursory view of the topographical features of the country to the south and southeast from a peak near our camp, and foreseeing that the farther my line of topography extended in that direction, toward what was known as the "head of the Amargosa," the position of which point was very indefinite and mythical, the greater would be the probability of my forming a junction with your line, without serious difficulty on my outward march from Camp Independence to meet you subsequent to this time.

Dr. Hoffman and party having arrived on the 8th, the next day I ordered him with the same party to cross Clayton Valley in a southeasterly direction, cross the Montezuma Range into Alida Valley, moving south and southeasterly down that valley to Gold Mountain, visiting the mines there, and swing around the Palmetto Mountains to the westward, examining those mines, and thence to rejoin me in Fish Lake Valley.

I directed the chief topographer, Mr. Nell, to make a very careful survey of the country thus traversed, to fix as many points as possible to the south and southeast of Gold Mountain, and to collect every item of topographical and geographical information he could obtain in regard to that *terra incognita*. This he did with great ability and judgment, and to my entire satisfaction. The knowledge thus obtained was afterward of the greatest service.

On the 10th we crossed the Red Mountain Range to the north of Red Mountain and Silver Peak, the two most noted peaks of this range, and camped at Red Mountain Spring, near the foot of the former peak, on the western slope, having made a short march of eleven and three-fourths miles. From this point myself and a small party made the ascent of those peaks and took barometrical observations. The assistant topographer, Mr. Klett, also took advantage of this to gain an extended view of the country.

The next day the party moved to near Fish Lake, a small body of tepid water, a few rods in extent, in Fish Lake Valley, a distance of nineteen miles.

There is pretty good grazing in the Red Mountain Range, and plenty of timber for fuel on the mountain ridge and western foot-hills. Abundance of excellent water is found at three points on the western slope, at Red Mountain, Mamie, and Cave Springs. It is said that Mamie Spring has only been running about two years.

Red Mountain is of volcanic origin, as is also Silver Peak. These two peaks are about three miles apart and joined by a sharp, comb-like ridge. The western foot-hills are of sedimentary origin.

From Fish Lake Valley to Camp Independence there is nothing new of topographical importance, as our route lay sensibly along an area surveyed by Professor Whitney in his able geological survey of the State of California.

At Fish Lake Dr. Hoffman and party joined, returning from Gold Mountain. His report is appended, marked C, and he was immediately detached to make a side trip to the northward via Columbus, thence, crossing the White Mountains to McBride's ranch, he was to follow down Owen's River and valley to the rendezvous camp at Camp Independence examining the mines and mining districts on his route. His report of this trip is appended hereto, marked D.

There are several ranches in Fish Lake Valley; hay, barley, oats, and potatoes being produced in abundance. Irrigation is necessary. Near the south end of the valley is Piper's ranch, the most important one, perhaps, in the valley, several hundred acres being under cultivation, and irrigated by the waters of Cottonwood Creek. Quite a large area could be rendered productive by a judicious use of the water from small creeks issuing from the White Mountains, which are soon lost in the sand. A good wagon-road connects Piper's ranch with Palmetto, and another with Deep Spring Valley.

From Fish Lake we marched to Piper's ranch, twenty-two miles, thence crossing a low range through a good pass, and passed down the eastern side of Deep Spring Valley, a small interior basin about ten miles long by four or five miles wide, inclosed by two spurs of the White Mountains, which fork at the upper end of the valley and join again at the lower end, producing this unique basin. Three small lakes, a salt marsh, and several springs, some of the latter being sulphur springs, are situated at the southern extremity of the valley.

Wyoming Creek rises in the mountains to the northwest and running southeast for four or five miles sinks in the sand. Plenty of water and good grass at lower extremity of this valley, but no wood. The remainder of the valley is covered with sage-brush, growing in a deep, sandy soil.

From Deep Spring we crossed the White Mountains into Owen's River Valley through a very good natural pass, but which, at two points, is impracticable for wagons. A wagon-road is being constructed from Owen's River up the western slope, which will descend into Deep Spring Valley by a cañon to the north of the one by which we ascended. Plenty of wood for fuel on and near the summit. Distance to Owen's River about twenty-two miles.

We crossed the river at a ford above and near Big Pine Creek, which is a very good one when the river is not too high. There are several ranches here on Big Pine Creek, but a great deal more land could be irrigated and reclaimed, as the supply of water in this creek is exceedingly abundant and excellent, and has a good deal of fall.

At this point I left my train to follow me on next day, and pushed forward to Camp Independence, about twenty-eight miles distant, where it also arrived the 18th, at 10.30 a. m. Here I immediately established an astronomical and meteorological station, and placed Mr. Austin, the astronomer, in charge. Mr. A. R. Marvine reporting here to me, was assigned as assistant to Mr. Austin, as previously directed by you.

FROM CAMP INDEPENDENCE TO GOLD MOUNTAIN AND RETURN.

Immediately upon my arrival at Camp Independence I fitted out a small party of picked men and carefully selected animals, to run a reconnaissance line to what was known as the head of the Amargosa. The object of this line was to determine whether or not a passage could be found directly to the eastward over the sterile deserts and mountains intervening between the Amargosa and Owen's Rivers that was practicable for a large train of men and animals; to procure data for constructing an accurate topographical map of that unknown area; to make collections in natural history, mineralogy, and geology; and, lastly, to form a junction, if possible, with your line, and, if a practicable route was discovered, to lead your large train to our rendezvous camp in Owen's River Valley. This party consisted of one topographer, two civilian assistants, two soldiers, a guide, a packer, an Indian, and myself, with four pack-mules.

Before starting I could get no definite information concerning the country to be traversed, and from every quarter received the most discouraging accounts of the dangers attending such a trip through a country entirely destitute of water, as far as known, after crossing the Inyo Range. Not deterred by these unfavorable reports, I was enabled to take the field again within three days after my arrival, with my animals re-shod, and the party supplied with forage and rations.

I would here state that I am deeply indebted to Major H. C. Egbert, captain Twelfth Infantry, commanding post of Camp Independence, and to Lieutenant W. E. Dove, Twelfth Infantry, acting assistant quartermaster at that post, for their prompt and energetic co-operation, by placing all the resources of the post at my disposal, and lending me their earnest assistance.

About noon, July 21, we left camp, and passing through the town of Independence, crossed Owen's River at Bend City, (now deserted,) and ascended the mountains through Mazourka Cañon. Fifteen miles up we camped at an excellent spring; grass and wood plenty. Next day crossed the range and camped in a deep, rugged cañon filled with blocks of granite, and very narrow, which we called Wheeler's Cañon. Here there was plenty of wood and water, but very little grass. Below us, and to the southward, lay Salinas Valley, a small interior basin, about twelve miles long, and from five to eight miles wide, containing salt-beds near its southern extremity. Mr. Hahn, the guide, now requested us to remain in camp one day while he would go in advance and see if there was enough water for the party at Grape-Vine Spring, which, he said, was about thirty-five or, perhaps, forty miles distant. He said he knew the route, and was positive we could reach that point in one day's march; but when questioned in regard to the locality of the pass in the opposite range, he gave evasive answers, nor could he give any definite information in regard to the character of the country to be traversed.

From several previous interviews I had held with him in regard to this country, I had grave doubts as to whether he knew the country or not; these doubts were now painfully confirmed. Mr. Hahn asserted positively that he could go to Grape-Vine and return the same night by 10 p. m. I concluded to remain in camp one day and let him go in advance, directing him to be back by 2 a. m. the morning following, but that I should start on his trail at 5 a. m. whether he returned or not. I ordered Koehler and the Indian, "Sam," to go with him to Grape-Vine Spring and remain there, making collections in natural history till I came up.

July 24, at 5 a. m., Hahn not returning, I set out upon his trail to the northeast, hoping to meet him. This trail led over a rocky, volcanic divide, separating Salinas from Termination Valley, which latter was some fifteen or twenty miles long, having heavy sand-hills, over which the trail led, the mules sinking knee-deep at every step. The day was excessively hot. The wind, passing over the heated sand-hills, came in scorching gusts, rendering our sufferings intense and our thirst almost intolerable, while the incessant glare of the sun upon the white sand nearly blinded us and caused great pain in our eyes and heads after the first few hours. At 4 p. m. we struck the slope leading up to the foot-hills, covered with sharp rocks and jasper flints. By 5 p. m. we were brought to a halt half way up a sharp peak, over which the trail led, by the mules becoming so weak as to be unable to proceed farther. I ascended the peak alone on foot to get a view of the country beyond. Once up, I saw no hope of getting my animals, in their then weak and exhausted state, over the summit at this point, so steep and rocky were the mountains. Beyond, range after range of black ridges, their wall-like sides banded with white, red, and yellow strata, reared their frowning crests, and seemed to interpose an impassable barrier to farther progress. I returned to my anxious followers and we descended in silence and tried two or three cañons, but, after penetrating a short distance in each, were compelled to turn back by vertical walls of rock that effectually prevented our ascent. Worn out and almost exhausted, we bivouacked on the heated, flinty surface to get a little rest; made some coffee, our only fuel being some small bushes, and ate a little hard-tack. We dared not eat any meat for fear of increasing our thirst. I was surprised at the rapidity with which the mules weakened and succumbed to fatigue upon this day's march. We saw nothing of Hahn, and I concluded that he had found the country worse than he anticipated, and had, no doubt, deserted us; or, thinking, perhaps, we would not attempt to follow his trail with pack-mules over such a country, had gone on to join you. Twenty-four miles were made this day. Most of the distance we had to march on foot, owing to the weakness of our animals. The soles of my shoes had completely worn out, and the others were but little better off. Fortunately, I had a pair of slippers with me, which protected my already bleeding and lacerated feet a little at least.

Next morning I started off to southward along the foot-hills, to make one last endeavor to find a pass through which I could penetrate this range into the valley I knew must lie beyond. Happily

11

I found a cañon which bade fair to lead us to the summit without serious obstacle. This we called Last Hope Cañon. We reached the summit without difficulty, and here found the trails of the three animals ridden by Koehler, Hahn, and the Indian. It was at or near this point that Koehler afterward told me he had last seen Hahn about 8 p. m., at which time Hahn turned and left him without saying a word, and that he called to him but received no answer, and supposed he had gone back to meet me. Hahn must have followed after Koehler and the Indian that night, for we found the three trails lower down and near the mouth of the cañon. This trail we followed eagerly down a deep cañon, but scarcely had we proceeded half a mile ere we came upon one of those falls of tilted slate which so often impede or prevent one's progress in these cañons. With considerable loss of time we succeeded in reaching the arroyo below by climbing a bluff and going down a steep incline of loose rocks and soil, but hardly half a mile more had been traversed before we came upon another fall, about 30 feet high. This barrier appeared at first sight to be impossible to surmount with our loaded pack-mules, but to return was hopeless, for the mules were too weak to climb back around the first fall. Our situation was indeed critical. Here we drank the last drop of water that we had husbanded carefully, amounting to only a few swallows each. This appeared rather to increase than alleviate our burning thirst. The party looked at me in silence till I gave the order for unpacking and lowering the cargoes with lash-ropes over the precipice. This was done cheerfully and without a murmur. With much labor, patience, and coaxing we got the mules to clamber up the cliffs and slide down into the wash below, without the loss of a single animal.

I cannot speak in too high terms of the admirable courage and cheerful obedience of my little party during this trying day. Feeling little hope of meeting with water, we moved silently down for several miles, when suddenly a cry of "water" was heard from the man in front, who pointed to a small green patch on the mountain-slope to the northwest.

At the mouth of this cañon—called Break Neck Cañon by the men—we left the trail of the men who had preceded us, they having turned off to the right, and made for the green spot over a perfect net-work of rocky ravines. The surface was completely covered with broken volcanic rocks about the size of ordinary cobble-stones. About sundown we reached it, and found water sufficient for our wants by digging. Our joy at this discovery knew no bounds. This we christened "Last Chance Spring." Distance made from last camp, nineteen miles.

The next day, feeling very foot-sore and weak, though much refreshed, we started across the upper end of Death Valley, traveling over a gravelly, sandy desert to Gold Mountain, twenty-two and a half miles distant, reaching there about 4 p. m. About the middle of the valley we crossed a mule-track leading north toward Tule Cañon; this we thought to be the track of Hahn's mule.

At Gold Mountain, finding two miners, I learned from them that I could not reach the Amargosa in less than three days' march, owing to the worn-out and lame condition of my animals. This would render me too late to meet you at that point according to our preconcerted arrangement. I prevailed upon Mr. T. J. Shaw, one of the miners, to take a fresh mule of his own and carry a message to you the next night. He did so, and returned the night following, bringing back your answer, which informed me of the critical condition of your party in regard to provisions, and also of the non-arrival of Hahn, the guide.

This latter advice led me to suppose that he had deserted us to our fate, and made for Tule Cañon, where there was water. I immediately sent Mr. Shaw back to Grape-Vine to guide your train to Pigeon Spring, via Death Valley and Tule Cañon, while, with my party, I started for Fish Lake Valley to get supplies, and returned to Pigeon Spring, which we accomplished by 6 a. m. on the morning of the 28th, having been twenty hours in the saddle. That same day I went to the head of Death Valley to meet the train, but failing to make it out on the desert, returned, and had just laid down to obtain a little rest when Mr. Shaw arrived with a note from Dr. Cochrane, who was in charge, saying that they had arrived in a very exhausted condition at Tule Spring, some eight or nine miles distant. I immediately saddled up, and taking some flour and barley, set out for that point, reaching there at 2.30 a. m.

The next day I moved your train over the mountains to Pigeon Spring, where, killing a beef, and having plenty of wood, grass, and water, we enjoyed a good night's rest and the first hearty meal either party had had for several days. Thence, by easy marches, via Piper's ranch and Deep Spring Valley, I reached the rendezvous camp.

FROM CAMP INDEPENDENCE TO COTTONWOOD SPRINGS, NEVADA.

During the time that we lay in Independence I was engaged in fitting out and supplying the different parties with subsistence stores, preparatory to another forward movement, and in duties of a general executive nature.

August 12, main party No. 1 left this camp and moved south through Independence and Lone Pine, crossing Owen's River and camping near its mouth after a march of twenty miles. At this point you left us, and passing via Cerro Gordo were going to run a reconnaissance line to the north of mine, and then join me in the Telescope Range.

Our next march was to the east of Owen's Lake, some twelve miles, to a point below Swansea; road very sandy; short alkali grass, very poor in quality; bad water, and no wood. We then moved southeast to near Arab Springs, in the Coso Range, about sixteen miles. Here we had plenty of wood and grass, but very little water, though plenty of water was found at a large spring, five miles distant, in east side of range. The next day we crossed a small, broken, desert valley, called Tortoise Valley, and camped twenty-five miles out, near Egan's Falls, in Darwin Cañon; little wood, plenty of water, but no grass here. The spring here suddenly rises near the foot of a high bluff, and quite a little stream issues forth; running a short distance, it is precipitated over several cascades, from 12 to 80 feet high, formed by slate ledges. The cañon at this point, and for some distance below, was impracticable, being only a narrow gorge cut through the slate by the water. The formation of this range is chiefly granite, slate, and volcanic rocks, with large mineral deposits in Granite Mountains. From here we crossed a high mountain by a steep trail, and, passing to the north and west of Granite Mountain, we regained Darwin Cañon, and following it down we debouched from the Tortoise Range into Panamint Desert, a sterile basin, utterly destitute of vegetation except a few thorny shrubs. This desert for some miles was sandy. Then crossing a large alkali flat, till near the eastern side, our route lay over low volcanic mesas whose surfaces were torn up and washed into deep, rocky ravines by the terrific water-spouts which are of frequent occurrence in this section. The trail now was extremely rough and rocky, rendering traveling very difficult; reaching the foot-hills we suddenly changed our direction from southeast to northeast, and proceeded up Rose Cañon seven or eight miles to Rose Springs, about five miles northwest of Telescope Peak, on the western slope of Telescope Range, where we camped. The weather was extremely hot, men and animals suffering greatly from thirst and fatigue.

Panamint Desert is between twenty and thirty miles in length, and from eight to eighteen miles wide, a desolate waste of sand, gravel, alkali flats, and low mesas, with shifting sand-hills near northern extremity. Horned rattlesnakes met with here. Telescope Range, to the eastward from where we entered the desert, presented that peculiar banded structure of bright colors, known among old prospectors as " calico ranges."

Town's Pass lay to the north of our camp. At Rose Spring we had plenty of water, and near the head of the cañon, which was an open plateau, plenty of grass and wood. Here we lay for a few days to send a topographical party to the top of Telescope Peak, and pursuant to your verbal instructions I dispatched Mr. Charles King to Furnace Creek, on the east side of Death Valley, to seek a pass over the range and across that valley, and also to ascertain the amount of water there. This he succeeded in doing with great judgment. I also dispatched Mr. Egan, the guide, who so kindly volunteered to lead us to this point, with two men to go to Cottonwood Cañon, some distance up the range, there to meet and conduct you to my camp.

On the morning of August 19 he left them and went on ahead to the northward, up the west side of Death Valley, to find that cañon, and, having an excellent mule, was soon out of sight.

They followed his trail till 11 a. m., and found their mules failing so fast that they turned back to Marble Spring, a place they had passed the day before. After much suffering and fatigue they regained my camp. As Mr. Egan had appeared quite positive in his knowledge of the location of the point designated to meet you, I had not the slightest doubt but that he had reached the camp of the small party at that place; but to guard against any chances of his failure to reach that point, and in case he should return to Marble Spring, I sent a man to the latter place with a note, advising him of our movement (should he not find the broad trail of the main party) across Death Valley, and also sent rations to be left there for him.

Upon this day you rejoined me and assumed command of the party. As Mr. Egan could not have reached Cottonwood before you left, we concluded that he had joined them afterward. I had no apprehensions for his safety, because he seemed perfectly conversant with the country. However, rations and a note were left for him at Rose Spring in case he *should* return to that place. Several days after, when the side party from Cottonwoods joined us at Ash Meadows, I learned that Mr. Egan had never joined them, and was supposed to have lost himself in Death Valley. Intelligence has since been received that he was heard from in Clarke District, near the Colorado.

From Rose Spring to Ash Meadows, Nevada, my duties were chiefly of a military nature, having command of the escort, and in executive charge of the train under your immediate direction.

The route between these two points lay, the first day, along and over the Telescope Range to Death Valley Cañon; the next, Death Valley was crossed at a point where it was some fifteen or eighteen miles wide. This crossing was made safely, a small side party being detached to take meteorological observations at the lowest part or sink of the valley, about ten miles to the right, and southward. We camped at Furnace Creek on the east side of the valley. Wood scarce, grass poor in quality, being short, alkali grass, very enervating to animals; water plenty, coming from numerous warm springs.

Two days' hard marching brought our worn-out train to Ash Meadows, where we found plenty of excellent grass and water, the latter from warm springs. Very little wood here. To reach this point we had to cross the Funeral Mountains, a range quite high and steep, and the Amargosa Desert, through which, for miles, the dry bed of the river of that name meanders southward. At this point we lay for a few days while you pushed forward to the rendezvous camp and sent back forage, of which we stood in great need. I then moved southward and crossed a low range into another sandy and gravelly desert, (Pah-rimp Desert,) which extends south for miles, and skirts the Spring Mountain Range. This desert contains several beautiful little oases, the principal one being at Pah-rimp Springs, at which point are located quite a number of Pah-Ute Indians, very friendly and quite intelligent. These Indians raise corn, melons, and squashes. Great quantities of wild grapes were found around these springs. From here, another day's march brought us to Stump Spring, on the old California emigrant-road. This road we followed to the rendezvous camp at Cottonwood Springs, Nevada, crossing the Spring Mountain Range, through an excellent pass near Mountain Spring, where we found plenty of wood, grass, and water.

At Cottonwood Springs we lay for several days, procuring supplies from Camp Mohave and Las Vegas. Here the river party was detached to make the ascent of the Colorado by boat, and Lieutenant Lockwood placed in command of the land parties.

FROM COTTONWOOD SPRINGS TO SAINT THOMAS, NEVADA.

On the 15th of September, Lieutenant Lockwood left this rendezvous camp for Las Vegas, twenty-two miles distant, and ordered me to follow with my party twenty-four hours later. At Las Vegas we lay a day or two, awaiting the arrival of our supplies from Camp Mohave.

On the 20th we started on the arduous march across the Vegas plains and mountains to the old California crossing of the Muddy, about forty-five miles distant. This march was made at night, Lieutenant Lockwood and party leading. I followed with main party No. 1 about an hour later. We arrived next morning at the crossing. The following day we moved down to Saint Thomas, near the confluence of the Muddy with the Virgin.

At this point I was detached with a small topographical party to visit Salt Mountain, five miles south of Saint Thomas, and thence to proceed eastward across the Virgin Range to seek a point convenient to the crossing, for a rendezvous camp. The pass through this range is a very good one, practicable for wagons, though near the summit heavy sand was met with. The Mormons had passed through it formerly with their light wagons.

Two days' march brought us to Pah-Koon Springs, situated in a deep wash, which lies west of what the Mormons call the Grand Wash. The tract of country lying between the Virgin Range and the Se-Vitch Mountains to the eastward, and extending from near Saint George, Utah, to the Colorado River, is a high volcanic mesa, cut by numerous cañons, very deep, but nearly all of which empty into the Grand Wash. Getting into these chasms once, it is almost impossible to get out for miles, the walls being high bluffs and nearly vertical. These cañons, or arroyos, rise to the northward in large upland plateaus, densely covered with cedar, containing a good deal of grass, but very little water.

Pah-Koon Springs are nine in number, all warm, with beds of quicksand beneath. The Indians have small patches of ground here which they irrigate and cultivate during the seasons they have no pine-nuts.

From Pah-Koon Springs we marched northward for a day, a night, and portion of next day, up one of these deep cañons, till we reached the elevated plateau covered with cedar, grass, and Spanish bayonets, where we found a small spring affording only a few quarts of water; thence crossing the Virgin Range and following down Rattlesnake Cañon, we reached the Rio Virgin. A march of eighteen miles in the bed of the river brought us to Lieutenant Lockwood's camp.

The formation was generally sandstone, overlapped by basaltic lava. The plateaus have a red soil, due, principally, to the disintegration of the bright-red sandstone.

The Mormons have a large stock-range here, there being sufficient water during most seasons.

FROM SAINT GEORGE TO THE CROSSING OF THE COLORADO.

October 1, Lieutenant Lockwood, with Mr. Spencer, the guide, and two men, left our camp near Saint George, and started for the crossing at the mouth of the Big Cañon of the Colorado, to make preliminary preparations for crossing that river, and left me in command of both land parties, with orders to follow as rapidly as possible. This I did, reaching Pah-Koon Springs on the evening of the 3d. It was intended to send a small topographical party down the Grand Wash, with orders to cross over and join me at Pah-Koon Springs, but, upon reflection, I concluded I could find a shorter, and perhaps better route, by going down the Grand Wash with the main

parties, and crossing the mesa to the eastward of my former line. The only difficulty I apprehended was in not being able to descend the abrupt bluffs from the mesa into Pah-Koon Wash.

The Mormons penetrated down the Grand Wash to the Colorado, with wagons, some years
ago. We found no obstacle that could not easily be overcome, and after following the Grand
Wash for about twelve miles, rose up on the mesa and had an excellent road across it, which
commanded a view to and beyond the Colorado. We had to enter this wash again lower down,
following which for a few miles we crossed the mesa to the southwest, and found no difficulty in
getting off it and reaching Pah-Koon Springs. At this point we found orders left by Lieutenant
Lockwood to lie over one day.

Plenty of water, little grass, and no wood except mesquite, here. The next night I received an
order from you, stating that you had completed the junction with your river party, and ordering
me to push forward as rapidly as possible the next day, and try to arrive there in time to cross
Lieutenant Lockwood's train the same day.

A trail led from Pah-Koon Springs to the old Ute crossing, about twenty-eight miles in
length, passing water twice on the route; but learning that a very steep bluff had to be ascended
from the Grand Wash, where we would have to unpack and take up half-loads at a time, which
would cause great delay, I attempted to get on the mesa higher up the wash, and succeeded
without difficulty. The route I took was much shorter, but very heavy and sandy in places, with
several steep inclines, as my trail led over a succession of washes and ravines, running southwesterly into the Grand Wash. Striking the head of a cañon which led almost direct to the
crossing, we arrived there before sundown, and before 9 p. m. had everything crossed by the boats
except the mules, which were swum over next morning. Lieutenant Lockwood superintended
the crossing in person.

The distance from this point to Truxton Springs was traversed in four days, both main land
parties moving together, with Lieutenant Lockwood in command. Arriving here, we found that
our supplies had not reached this point from Camp Mohave. Lieutenant Lockwood immediately
dispatched two Army wagons, belonging to the new escort, a detachment of Troop C, Third Cavalry,
which we found encamped here, for them. These supplies came promptly to hand, thanks to the
energy of Lieutenant C. P. Eagan, Twelfth Infantry, assistant commissary of subsistence at that
post. I was sent with three men to Camp Hualapais, about eighty miles distant, for the mail and
some additional supplies.

FROM TRUXTON SPRINGS TO PRESCOTT, VIA CAMP DATE CREEK AND BRAD-SHAW MOUNTAINS.

October 26 I was detached, with a small topographical party and a picked escort of fifteen
men, to move in a southeasterly direction to Camp Date Creek, thence to go to Bradshaw Mountains, visiting the mining districts there, and move northward to Prescott, Arizona Territory. A
few miles north of Truxton Springs I gained the mesa which is a continuation of the grand Colorado
plateau, and made old Camp Willow Grove that night. The country from this point was almost
entirely unknown; our guide, Mr. Spencer, had been down to the Santa Maria once before, but we
did not follow the trail he had before traveled, though we crossed it several times.

The stretch of country lying between the Aquarius Mountains on the west, and the Juniper
Mountains on the east is, after the first twelve or fifteen miles south of Willow Grove, which is
very rough and broken, a high, rolling, grassy mesa, abounding in antelope and deer; having
plenty of excellent water in the creeks which lie at the bottoms of deep ravines, called in that
country "box cañons," from their walls being so abrupt. These cañons are from 100 to 1,200 feet

deep, with walls of volcanic rock, almost vertical, and after once reaching their beds it is an impossibility to get out except at a very few points; this is especially the case toward the lower ends. The creeks abound in excellent trout.

Trout Creek is the principal tributary of the Big Sandy, rising near Aztec Pass, in the Juniper Mountains; flowing southwest, it drains a large scope of country south of Willow Grove and enters the Big Sandy, after passing a narrow, rocky gorge cut through the Aquarius Mountains.

To the south of Trout Creek is a low, rolling divide, or water-shed, separating the waters of Big Sandy from those of the Santa Maria.

We crossed a number of these box cañons in succession, near their heads, the only place we could cross them. Through the principal ones flowed Ah-ha-pook, Spencer's, Sycamore, and Yavapais Creeks, all tributaries of the Santa Maria. Through this section we found small bands of Apache-Mohave Indians, and at Yavapais Creek quite a large band, well armed with rifles and well supplied with food. The head chief appeared quite friendly, but the young bucks looked upon us with no favorable eye. We had no trouble with them, however, and the next day crossed the sandy bed of the Santa Maria River, near the junction of its three forks, all of which were dry, except in one a stagnant pool was found, in which tules were growing. We then crossed a high granite range to the southeast, called the Santa Maria Range, into Date Creek Valley. This valley has a light, sandy soil, and contains considerable grass. The military post of Camp Date Creek is situated on a low mesa, south of the creek. All the officers of the post generously extended to us their assistance, and the hospitalities of the camp. To the eastward lies Antelope Valley, a nearly circular basin of high altitude, from which it is divided by a range of mountains, principally granite. To the north and northeast lie Thompson, Skull, and Kirkland Valleys.

From Date Creek we crossed the range to the east, and camped one day in Antelope Valley. From this point I sent my pack-train to Prescott, under the command of Sergeant T. J. Moore, Troop C, Third United States Cavalry, and next day crossed a low, rocky range to the eastward, covered with dense *chaparral*, and entered Walnut Grove, a settlement on Hassyampa Creek, where we found cultivated farms.

Following down this valley, along a wagon-road, by a circuitous route we reached Minnehaha Flat, a densely timbered plateau on the west slope of the Bradshaw Mountains. The next morning we reached Bradshaw City, about five miles farther east, by a steep mountain trail.

This mining camp has an altitude of about 7,000 feet. After visiting the mines we proceeded north along this range, passing through the Tiger, Pine Grove, Bradshaw, and Turkey Creek mining districts. The Bradshaw Range is densely timbered with excellent pine. Mineral deposits are found all along this range, but have not been developed. Plenty of water was found at Date Creek, in Antelope Valley, Walnut Grove, but very little in the Bradshaw Mountains or Turkey Creek.

FROM PRESCOTT, ARIZONA TERRITORY, TO TUCSON, ARIZONA TERRITORY, VIA CAMP APACHE.

Leaving Prescott, Arizona Territory, main party No. 1, commanded by yourself, proceeded to Camp Apache, via San Francisco Mountains, and through the Great Tonto Basin, arriving there November 25. We delayed at this point one day to obtain supplies, and from there proceeded by rapid, forced marches, to Camp Grant and Tucson, at which latter place the expedition was disbanded and the field operations ceased.

My duties during this trip were principally of a military character, being in command of the escort and in executive charge of the party. I also had charge of the meteorological observations, and assisted in the astronomical work.

RECAPITULATION.

The length of the reconnaissance line surveyed under my immediate direction is nine hundred and eighteen miles, embracing an area of 11,750 square miles; this is independent of the line and area included in the trip from Owen's Lake to the west side of Death Valley, and from Ash Meadows to Cottonwood, Nevada. These lines were carefully measured with Cassella's field transits; all important points on both sides being established by triangulation. The base-lines used were the odometer measurements between the topographical stations, carefully reduced. Astronomical observations were taken at as many camps as practicable, to serve as checks for connecting the transit work. The distances from Belmont to Camp Independence, on both the main and side lines, were carefully measured with odometers, as also were those from Saint Thomas to Salt Mountain and return, from Saint Thomas to Saint George, Utah, and thence to the crossing of the Colorado.

The distances from Truxton Springs to Prescott, Arizona Territory, via Camp Date Creek and Bradshaw Mountains, were estimated.

Meteorological observations were taken at every camp, and hourly stations established at all rendezvous camps. Observations with aneroid barometers were taken at every topographical station and camp, and carefully compared, daily, with cistern barometers, thereby furnishing data for determining a profile of the route traversed.

VALLEYS.

The valleys passed through were twenty-three in number, mostly north and south, viz: Monitor, Ralston, Big Smoky, Clayton, Fish Lake, Deep Spring, Alida, Palmetto, Owen's River, Salinas, Termination, Death, Tortoise, Panamint, Amargosa, Pah-rimp, the Grand Wash and tributaries, Trout Creek Basin, Santa Maria Basin, Date Creek, Antelope, Walnut Grove, and Turkey Creek.

MOUNTAINS.

The principal ranges were the Toquima, Toyabe, San Antonio, Lone Mountain, Red Mountain, Montezuma, Palmetto, Green Mountain, Gold Mountain, White Mountain, Inyo, Telescope, Coso, Tortoise, Funeral, Spring Mountain, Virgin, Juniper, Aquarius, Santa Maria, Antelope, and Bradshaw.

INDIANS.

The various tribes encountered were the Shoshones, Pah-Utes, Owen's River Indians, Se-Vitch, See-Vints, Hualapais, and Yavapais, or Apache-Mohaves.

The Shoshones were scattered sparsely from Belmont to Fish Lake Valley, in the Toyabe, Red, and Montezuma Mountains. A small band was seen east of Palmetto, about Tule Springs.

The Pah-Utes were found at Piper's ranch, in the White Mountains and Deep Spring Valley, and afterward in considerable numbers around Pah-rimp Springs, Cottonwoods, and Las Vegas, Nevada.

The Owen's River Indians are scattered along that valley, but of their numbers I could get no definite idea. They are not very numerous.

The Se-Vitches are few in number and live in the mountains adjacent to the Grand Wash and its tributaries. They have little communication with the whites.

The Hualapais, formerly a numerous and warlike tribe, are now much reduced in numbers, and are at peace with the whites. They are found in the Hualapais and Aquarius Mountains, and around Truxton, Beale's, and Peacock's Springs, and on the Big Sandy.

The Yavapais, or Apache-Mohaves, are quite numerous, and range over a great extent of country, from Willow Grove and Aztec Pass, south to Fort Yuma and below Wickenburgh; from Bill Williams's Fork east to the Tonto Basin. They are broken into many small bands. I only saw about five hundred or six hundred of them. At Ash Meadows is a small band of about fifty men, women, and children, composed of renegade Shoshones and Pah-Utes, together with a mixture of these two tribes.

Most of these Indians lead a precarious life, subsisting upon pine-nuts, the fruit of the piñon pine, the seeds of weeds and grasses which they carefully collect, jack-rabbits, lizards, small birds, and the few deer they are able to find occasionally in the mountains.

The Pah-Utes in Pah-rimp Valley, and around Cottonwoods and Las Vegas, raise, in addition, corn, melons, squashes, and gather large quantities of wild grapes, which grow abundantly near the springs. They are quite intelligent, and were very friendly. Virtue is almost unknown among them, and syphilitic diseases very common.

The Apache-Mohaves were by far the most superior Indians met with, being well armed, well equipped with food and clothing and blankets. Their country abounds in deer and antelope, and in all their wigwams were found large stores of dried venison, grass-seed, from which they make a kind of bread, and dried "tunas," as they call the prickly pear that grows in great abundance in their country. The muscular development of these Indians, and especially of their lower extremities, is truly wonderful. The women are often beautiful, and, as a class, are strictly chaste and virtuous, any deviation from the path of rectitude being visited by the summary punishment of cutting off the nose, from their jealous lords and masters.

AGRICULTURAL LANDS

are few and limited in extent, the greater part of the area surveyed being characterized by almost perfect sterility. The tillable oases are found in Fish Lake, Deep Spring, Owen's River, at Ash Meadows in Amargosa Desert, Pah-rimp, Date Creek, Antelope, and Walnut Grove Valleys.

GRAZING LANDS.

Stock-ranges, like agricultural lands, are far from being numerous and extensive. A limited amount of grass was found in the Red Mountains. The White Mountains are said to possess a tolerable range. Other grazing lands were found at Palmetto, Deep Springs, along Owen's River, at Ash Meadows, head of the Grand Wash, around Tin-na-kah, and Truxton Springs, and on the mesa between the Aquarius and Juniper Mountains.

At Palmetto, near Pigeon Spring, there are over 5,000 acres of very good grazing lands, with plenty of water.

The finest stock-range and grass-lands met with on my lines were those upon the high, rolling mesa south of Willow Grove, inhabited by the Apache-Mohaves, which embrace thousands of acres, with plenty of clear running water in the creeks that flow through the "box cañons."

MINING DISTRICTS.

Twenty-four mining districts lay upon the lines traversed by the parties under my direction, viz: San Antonio, Montezuma, Palmetto, Alida, Gold Mountain, Green Mountain, Columbus, Oneata, Blind Spring, Montgomery, Silver Peak, Red Mountain, Deep Spring Valley, Fish Spring, Granite Mountain, Tiger, Pine Grove, Bradshaw, Turkey Creek, Weaver, Walnut Grove, Hassyampa, Martinez, and Santa Maria districts. For notices of these, your attention is respectfully invited to my report on "Mines and Mining Districts," appended and marked A, and to Dr. W. J. Hoffman's reports, marked, respectively, B, C, and D.

12

MEANS OF COMMUNICATION.

On the completion of the road over the White Mountains to Deep Spring Valley, a very fair wagon-road will exist from Belmont to Owen's River, California. From Gold Mountain, Fish Lake Valley is reached by a tolerable trail to Palmetto, and from there to Piper's ranch by wagon-road. A good road could be constructed the entire distance without great difficulty.

Silver Peak is connected with Montezuma, San Antonio, and Fish Lake Valley by wagon-roads, and by the latter road, via Columbus, with Wadsworth, on the Central Pacific Railroad. From Columbus a road leads over the White Mountains to Owen's River; thence down that valley to Independence and Lone Pine. A wagon-road can be constructed from Montezuma to Gold Mountain, via Alida Valley. That a road can be constructed from Saint George, Utah, down through the Grand Wash and its tributaries, via Pah-Koon Springs, crossing the Colorado at or near the "old Ute crossing," and thence via Tin-na-kah and Truxton Springs to Camp Hualapal and Prescott, Arizona Territory, there can be no doubt; for a discussion of the practicability of the route, I would respectfully invite attention to Lieutenant Lockwood's report.

REMARKS.

This report is necessarily chiefly narrative in its nature, and is, perhaps, not so concise and positive as it might be, owing to the fact that a great many of the field-notes shipped have not arrived, being blockaded and delayed while *en route* by the severe snow-storms on the Union Pacific Railroad. In it I have only presented information in regard to the area explored and surveyed entirely under my direction, leaving those portions upon which I only *assisted* to be treated of by yourself and Lieutenant Lockwood.

Every effort was made to make the collections in natural history, mineralogy, and geology as full and comprehensive as possible.

The greatest care was taken to render the geographical and topographical notes full, clear, and explicit, in order that the final map would present all the essential details of the physical conformation of the area explored.

It was found that the general trend of the mountain ranges encountered was northwest and southeast, separated by elongated valleys, which are often broken into two or more parts or lesser valleys, by lateral spurs diverging from the main ranges. These valleys are nearly all arid deserts, small interior basins with no surface outlet for their waters, resembling often the dry beds of lakes, and are component parts of the great interior basin.

The water-sheds of these basins, the constitution of their soils, their geological and physical characteristics, the distribution of vegetation and water, together with their properties and amount, have been carefully noted, and will appear in a general report intended to embrace all the detailed information upon these various subjects.

Too much praise and commendation cannot be bestowed upon the detachment of Troop I, Third United States Cavalry, who acted as escort to the expedition during the entire term of field operations.

I would here thank all the members of the expedition under my charge, for the able and efficient manner in which they performed their various duties, and the earnest interest manifested by them in the success of the expedition.

Respectfully submitted.

D. A. LYLE,
Second Lieutenant, Second United States Artillery.

Lieutenant GEORGE M. WHEELER,
United States Engineers, in charge of Explorations in Nevada and Arizona, Washington, D. C.

APPENDIX C.

REPORT OF EDWARD P. AUSTIN, ASTRONOMICAL ASSISTANT.

ENGINEER OFFICE, (EXPLORATIONS IN NEVADA AND ARIZONA,)
Washington, D. C., March 2, 1872.

SIR: I have the honor to submit the following preliminary report upon the astronomical operations for the determination of latitudes and longitudes, under my charge, during the season of 1871.

The stations occupied were Carlin, Nevada, and Battle Mountain, Nevada, on the Central Pacific Railroad, Austin, Nevada, Camp Independence, California, and Salt Lake, Utah.

The instruments employed were a sidereal chronometer by Negus, No. 1344; a mean solar chronometer by Hutton, No. 288; and a portable transit of 26-inch focus, and 1¾-inch aperture, by Würdemann, No. 16, which had been altered to convert it into a meridian instrument, similar to those introduced by the United States Coast Survey.

CARLIN, NEVADA.

Observations at Carlin consist in observations for time and exchanges of telegraphic signals for difference of longitude, with Washington, D. C., (United States Naval Observatory, J. R. Eastman, observer,) through Detroit, Michigan, (United States Lake Survey Observatory; O. B. Wheeler, observer,) on May 19, 23, and 24; and observations for latitude May 17, 25, 26, and 27.

BATTLE MOUNTAIN, NEVADA.

The observations at Battle Mountain include observations for time and exchanges of signals with Detroit, Michigan, June 1, 3, and 10; and observations for latitude, June 6, 7, 8, and 9.

AUSTIN, NEVADA.

At Austin, observations for time and exchanges of signals were made with Detroit and Washington, June 16, and with Detroit June 26, and 29.

Observations for latitude were made at this place June 15, 17, 21, and 23.

CAMP INDEPENDENCE, CALIFORNIA.

At this place I was assisted by Mr. A. R. Marvine. The observations at this point consisted in observations for time, moon culminations for longitude, observations to determine the constants of the instrument, and observations for latitude. They lasted from July 21 to August 7.

SALT LAKE CITY, UTAH.

I then repaired to Salt Lake City, Utah, to await the arrival of Mr. Marvine at Saint George, Utah, when observations were made for time, and signals exchanged between Salt Lake and Saint George, on September 13, 14, and 15.

During the interval between my arrival at Salt Lake and Mr. Marvine's arrival at Saint George, observations were made to determine the constants of the transit instrument.

The instruments used at Salt Lake were a mean-time chronometer, by Barrand, No. 22961; and a portable transit of 31 inches focal length, 2½-inch aperture, by William Würdemann, No. 19, which was firmly mounted on a sandstone pier, in the observatory erected in 1869 for the United States Coast Survey party; these instruments, and the observatory, being the property of Brigham Young, president of the Mormon church.

PROBABLE CHARACTER OF RESULTS.

From the preliminary reductions, the probable error of a time determination with the instrument used at the stations from Carlin to Independence is from $\pm 0.''02$ to $\pm 0.''04$, and the probable error of a single pair observed for latitude is $\pm 1.''37$, giving the probable error of a result depending on thirty pairs $\pm 0.''25$; on fifty pairs $\pm 0.''20$. These values will be considerably reduced by the final computations.

The time determinations at Salt Lake, owing to the larger size and greater stability of the instrument, as well as the more favorable conditions for observing, give a probable error much less, being less than $\pm 0.''01$.

Considering the character of the instruments, the means of recording, and the limited time allowed for the observations, the probabilities are that the results will prove highly satisfactory.

Very respectfully, yours,

E. P. AUSTIN,
Astronomical Observer.

Lieutenant GEORGE M. WHEELER,
United States Engineers, in charge of explorations.

APPENDIX D.

REPORT OF G. K. GILBERT, GEOLOGICAL ASSISTANT.

ENGINEER OFFICE, (EXPLORATIONS IN NEVADA AND ARIZONA,)
Washington, D. C., March 9, 1872.

DEAR SIR: In addition to the results of my own work, which was performed throughout the entire season of field duty, geological data were collected for limited periods by several gentlemen of the scientific corps. Mr. A. R. Marvine, serving in the double capacity of astronomer and geologist, was busied with geological examinations more especially during the latter half of the season, and will himself prepare the results of his labors for publication. Lieutenant D. A. Lyle, Dr. W. J. Hoffman, Mr. C. A. Ogden, and Mr. E. P. Austin have volunteered to contribute geological information in regard to some regions that I was unable to visit. Altogether the geological observations will be found to relate to about one-half of the lines of geographical exploration and survey. Keeping pace in our movements with rapidly executed geographical work, the geologists were unable to command the time necessary to the complete description of even the immediate line of travel, and the most we can claim to have accomplished is a reconnaissance of our field. Of this character essentially have been the labors of geologists attached to other exploring parties, and, indeed, the achievement of more thorough work in connection with exploration is neither possible nor, in every sense, desirable. I would not, of course, be understood that it will be unprofitable to make a careful and detailed survey of the geological structure and mineral resources of our whole territory, but that the first efficient step toward its accomplishment must be a cursory reconnaissance—a preliminary survey—with a view to obtain, at the earliest possible date, the broadest generalizations, the simplest and most comprehensive ideas in regard to the sequence and distribution of the rocks, to serve as a frame-work in which every later study of a locality or district may find its appropriate place. More than this, these primary generalizations, crude though they are, and subject to indefinite future modification, answer in the best feasible manner the most pressing demands of a region that must depend for its development on the understanding and appreciation of its mineral resources. The limits within which the discovery of the several precious and useful minerals may be anticipated, and beyond which they need not be sought, are indicated by the first and most comprehensive lines the geologist draws on his map; for they chiefly depend on broad distinctions that cannot fail to be made on the first examination.

Our field of operations has afforded us a view within the space of a single season of an unusual variety of geological features distributed over an immense area. Our southward progress, amounting to nearly seven hundred miles in a right line, was accomplished by a zigzag course that showed us a belt of country averaging one hundred miles in width, and expanded in one part to two hundred and fifty miles. Of a great portion of this region no geological description whatever has been written, but at several points it has been intersected by the lines of earlier geological exploration, the majority of which have crossed the country in an east and west direction. It has been our province to establish the connection, and measurably to fill out the intervals between them. The relations which our investigations sustain to those of Dr. Newberry, Dr. Antisell, M. Marcou and others, in Arizona; of Professor Whitney, Professor Blake and others, in California, and of the geologists of the Fortieth Parallel Survey, enable us to have a far better understanding of the phenomena presented by our field than would be possible if our work stood alone, and enhance in more than one way the value of the contribution we are able to make to the geological history of the continent.

Our work was facilitated, in a measure that can hardly be appreciated by persons unfamiliar with deserts, by the absence of trees and absence of soil that characterize the greater part of Nevada and Arizona. Not merely were rock exposures everywhere provided without search, but the view was in all directions unimpeded, and we could frequently see the limits of the different rocks beautifully delineated on the slopes of the distant mountains, revealing at a glance relations that in a fertile country would appear only as the results of extended and laborious investigation. This advantage, which we shared with all our collaborators in the interior of the continent, enabled us to obtain from what was within our reach no inconsiderable knowledge of what was merely in sight, and thus expand into a belt what might otherwise be a mere line of observation.

In the arrangement of the geological material for the final report, two needs are to be considered. By the resident, and by the traveler or geologist who shall follow in our steps, local details and exact localities, will be demanded; while the general reader, scientific or lay, will care only for the deductions that are of broadest application and such facts as are most important in their relations to the study of the continent. For this reason the report will be divided into two principal parts, of which the first (Chapters I–VIII) will record all observations of a local character in geographical, or rather itinerary order; and the second (Chapters IX–XVII) will contain a systematic arrangement and discussion of the results of our work.

The following schedule will serve to indicate the scope of the report:

CHAPTER I. *Halleck Station to Ophir Cañon.*—A portion of our travel in this interval was upon the belt traversed by the Fortieth Parallel Survey, and the latter part lay along a portion of the Toyabe Range, already described in the first published volume of the report of that corps.

CHAPTER II. *Ophir Cañon to Pioche, and Silver Cañon to Big Pine.*—This route carried us eastward over a succession of meridional ranges, nine or ten in number, and then obliquely back to a point one hundred and fifty miles farther south. With (apparently) two exceptions, these ranges consist of highly-inclined, stratified rocks, more or less metamorphosed, associated with granite, and flanked—in places even covered—by volcanic materials.

CHAPTER III. *Big Pine, in Owen's Valley, to Camp Mohave.*—Owen's Lake is surrounded by a series of deserted beaches, marking epochs in the gradual desiccation of the Great Basin. On the uppermost are lacustrine shells (*Anodonta*) in abundance, showing that the lake when 50 feet deeper was of fresh water. I found them on none of the lower beaches, and the alkaline water of the present lake appears to support insect life only. Concordantly it appears that the lake had then an outlet, discharging its surplus water southward, over what is still the lowest point of the rim. We followed the bed of this ancient river for thirty-five miles, and passed in sight of the broad depression east of Walker's Pass, in which it terminated, and where it formed, doubtless, a lake as briny and desolate as the one that now accumulates the saline constituents of Owen's River. From Owen's Valley we once more crossed obliquely the system of mountain ranges.

CHAPTER IV. *Camp Mohave, via the Colorado River, to the mouth of Diamond Creek.*—The cañons of Colorado, cutting down almost to the ocean level, give natural cross-sections of several ranges, and afford an opportunity to study on a grand scale the dislocations that accompany the upheaval of mountains. The geological section of the river bank exhibits at the east the undisturbed strata of the Colorado plateau with a thickness of one mile; toward the west, the dislocated masses of the same strata, forming a series of ridges with their upturned edges; and still farther, the granite nuclei and flanking schists and lavas of Virgin and Black Ranges.

CHAPTER V. *Diamond Creek to the Triplets, in San Carlos Valley*—Our course lay along the southern margin of the Colorado plateau, and in our repeated ascents and descents of its escarpment a number of sections were obtained, establishing the identity of the principal beds for a distance of three hundred miles.

CHAPTER VI. *Triplets to Tucson.*

CHAPTER VII. This and the following chapter will comprise the report of Mr. A. R. Marvine, who furnishes the following *résumé :*

"Chapter VII will contain some scattering observations between Independence, California, and Saint George, Utah, with a more continuous set of observations between the latter place and Camp Verde, Arizona Territory. From Saint George the course was south, the 'Grand Wash,' lying between the eastern, precipitous face of the Colorado plateau and the Virgin Mountains, being followed, and the Colorado River crossed. Here we ascended from the granite to the lower bench of the plateau, and, traveling south and east near the edge, descended again to the granite near Truxton Springs. Granite, with some metamorphic rocks, predominates from here to Verde, forming, near the latter, the Black Hills, and being covered in some localities by lava fields and one or two isolated remnants of the plateau. The 'mineral' veins of this region occur in the granite and metamorphic formation.

"CHAPTER VIII. *From Camp Verde to Tucson.*—The valley of the Verde River, at the camp, indicates the line of demarkation between the granite of the Black Hills and the horizontal sedimentary strata of the Colorado plateau, which is here called the Black Mesa. We at once ascended and proceeded eastward to the Little Colorado, crossing the large basaltic mass which occupies the central area, rests upon the sedimentary rocks, and seems to have been continued somewhat farther north, in the vicinity of San Francisco Mountain. At the Little Colorado we turned south and east, crossed the Mogollon Mountains, and descended through the upper strata of the mesa to Camp Apache. The Mogollon, and probably the White Mountains farther east, are extended basaltic masses, resting on the mesa top in the same manner as San Francisco Mountain and adjacent lava masses. From Apache to Florence the course was southeast, passing through the lower sedimentary rocks of the mesa into the mountainous and diversified granitic region of Eastern Arizona, and out upon the deserts of the Gila River. Turning southeast, we remained on these to Tucson."

CHAPTER IX. *On the structure and age of the mountains of the Great Basin.*

CHAPTER X. *On the valleys of the Great Basin; their character dependent on origin, amount of filling, and present conditions.*—The great majority are troughs between upheaved meridional ranges, partly filled by *detritus* (of subaqueous and subaerial deposition) from the adjacent mountains, and modified by floods of lava, that in numerous instances have connected parallel ridges and thus divided, more or less perfectly, the intervening valleys. In some of the lower areas, to which, in the gradual emergence of the continent, the sea had longest access, the valleys have been so completely filled as to connect with each other and constitute plains, through which the peaks (or the remnants) of the intervening ranges jut as "lost mountains."

CHAPTER XI. *On Erosion.*—Besides the general discussion of the phenomena, so profusely displayed along the entire route, this chapter will contain notes on the pot-holes of the Colorado, and on the curious rock-sculpture executed by particles of sand driven by wind and by water. Here, too, will find place an account of some supposed drift-gravels, resting on the margin of the Colorado plateau near the Tonto Basin, in latitude 35° north.

CHAPTER XII. *On the Water Supply.*—Treating of the relations of springs to geological features, and of the considerations which should govern search for water by boring.

CHAPTER XIII. *On the distribution and age of the Sedimentary Rocks.*—The fossiliferous beds, of which the age was determined by the expedition, range from the Primordial to the Upper Carboniferous, and rest unconformably on a series of highly crystalline schists, with associated granites. Fossils were obtained from about thirty-five localities, two-thirds of which gave conclusive evidence of their geological horizon.

CHAPTER XIV. *On the geology of the Colorado Plateau.*

CHAPTER XV. *On Volcanic Rocks and Mountains.*—The entire field of our exploration has been the scene of prolonged, or recurrent, volcanic activity, reaching down to so recent a period that it would be rash to assert that it has even now finally ceased. There is no extended mountain range from the sides of which lavas have not flowed, and some are for long distances buried under the material that has found vent along their lines of fracture. From the Timpahute Range westward to the Amargosa, the eastern boundary of Death Valley, a distance of seventy-five miles in a direct line, we traveled entirely on volcanic material, and there is reason to believe that the field stretches northward an equal distance. In this and some other areas north of the Colorado, rhyolitic and trachytic lavas predominate, and volcanic sands and tufas are conspicuous elements of the mass. Farther south, in the vicinity of the Colorado plateau, the latter are rarely seen, and basaltic lavas assume great prominence. The collection of volcanic products is large, and cannot fail, with study, to add something to the rapidly increasing store of facts in regard to the ordinal sequence of lavas.

CHAPTER XVI. *Economic Geology.*—To the difficult and important subject of the geological distribution of auriferous and argentiferous veins, and their relation to the mountain system and to the intruded rocks, we hope to contribute some facts of value.

Our report will record the occurrence and position of coal, salt, gypsum, and other economic minerals. The former has been discovered near Camp Apache in beds of Carboniferous age, and probably referable to the Coal Measures. The seam is of tolerable thickness, but has not been sufficiently developed to test its quality. It will probably prove to be of non-coking, bituminous coal.

CHAPTER XVII. *Paleontology.*—The fossils of the expedition will be placed, I am happy to state, in the skillful and experienced hands of Mr. F. B. Meek, who will study and report upon them.

In the geological collections, limited in extent by the circumstances of transportation, &c., great care was taken to represent the characteristic lithological features of the several geological provinces, the prevalent varieties of rock being studiously preferred to the locally exceptional.

I remain, sir, very truly yours,

G. K. GILBERT.

Lieutenant GEORGE M. WHEELER,
          United States Engineers.

DATE			